A Taste of Something Wild COOKBOOK

WITHDRAWN

By Richard M. Gauerke

Adventure Publications, Inc.
Cambridge, MN

This book is dedicated to my wife Jane.

Unselfish, giving and easy to love, she willingly shared, encouraged and let me be me to pursue my other passions in this life.

Book and Cover Design by Jonathan Norberg

Cover Photo by Michael Peterson

Copyright 2006 by Richard M. Gauerke

All rights reserved.

10 9 8 7 6 5 4 3 2

Published by
Adventure Publications, Inc.
820 Cleveland St. S
Cambridge, MN 55008
1-800-678-7006
www.adventurepublications.net
ISBN-13: 978-1-59193-146-1
ISBN-10: 1-59193-146-0
Printed in the U.S.A.

INTRODUCTION

Hunting and fishing have been paramount in my quest for a worthy and good life, and it's been a wild and exciting adventure. I've been fortunate to have shared in the knowledge, hospitality and camaraderie of other like-minded and motivated folks who are now my friends. We're respectful of our heritage and the wild creatures that share our planet. The ethics of this heritage dictate that every critter harvested is brought to the table as a feast worthy of the adventure.

Whether it's pan-frying arctic grayling beside the mighty Mackenzie River or tail-gating canned pheasant and crackers in the Dakotas, food cooked in a simple manner generally tastes its best. It must be noted, however, that camp cooks also like to show off, and I'm no exception.

Waking one's palate and senses to the wonderful goodness of food from the wild is as satisfying as a clean shot or landing a lunker with light tackle. I have many converts with satisfied appetites to my credit, and I cherish every one. Therefore, sharing these recipes with you carries on my firm conviction that the feast completes the adventure.

A Taste of Something Wild is the culmination of years of hobby cooking and the introduction of wild fish and game into many traditional dishes. I bring pasta to life with wild pacific salmon, incorporate zucchini with fresh peppers to create a wonderful baked walleye, and create an attractive, tasty vegetable medley with pheasant. My venison fillet with crab sauce and wild rice is the ultimate comfort food.

It's with a great sense of accomplishment that I pass this book along to you. Enjoy these recipes and relish the results. I know you'll be pleased to share your wild bounty with your friends and family just as I have!

Table of Contents

UPLAND GAME, DUCKS & GEESE

Ducks & Geese

FISH

Freshwater Fish

Upland Game, Ducks & Geese

A Few Helpful Hints about Wildfowl

Shotgunning for game birds can be one of the greatest sports available. With the return of CRP, upland game is plentiful even on public land, and the ambitious hunter will generally succeed. Add a well-trained dog and you'll enjoy the best this world has to offer. The tasty meals you will able to create are endless. Game birds are very versatile and it's not difficult to find something that will please everyone. Birds and wild rice are practically synonymous in my mind and taste buds so you will find them joined in many of these recipes. Responding to requests, you will also find recipes that use pasta for other scrumptious meals. Enjoy and eat hearty.

Tips for tasty bird dishes:

- After the shot, draw the bird as quickly and conveniently as possible. Temperatures above 40° are meat's worst enemy and the objective is not to retain the body heat.

- In hot weather be prepared by bringing coolers with ice.

- If a cooler is not available, do not pile birds on top of each other.

- Keep the birds out of direct sunlight in a well-ventilated place.

- When processing, wash hands and utensils with soap and water.

- Bloodshot meat should be cleaned and trimmed. Try to remove all pellets.

- Birds to be cooked or canned within 3 days may be stored in the refrigerator until ready.

- Freeze meat as quickly as possible while it is still in good condition.

- Packaging parts of cut-up birds (e.g., breasts, thighs, etc.) makes for more efficient meal planning and preparation.

- Invest in a vacuum sealer and use it often.

- Prior to cooking, thaw birds in the refrigerator. Any meat thawed in a microwave should be cooked immediately.

- Don't overcook your meat.

Upland Casserole

3 cups cooked breast meat of pheasant, partridge or turkey
2 tablespoons butter
1 bunch fresh broccoli
1 small onion, chopped
½ lb. sliced mushrooms
2 cans cream of chicken soup
1 cup mayonnaise
1 teaspoon lemon juice
1 cup soft croutons
½ cup shredded cheddar cheese

Steam or boil the birds until meat is tender. Cool and remove any bones. Cut meat into bite-sized portions. Grease a 9x13 baking pan with butter. Rinse broccoli, remove the large leaves and heavy bottom stalk. Cut broccoli lengthwise from the head through the stalk. Arrange broccoli, onion, mushrooms and meat in pan. Blend soup, mayonnaise and lemon juice and pour over meat and veggies. Top with bread croutons, sprinkle with cheese. Bake uncovered for 25–30 minutes at 350°.

Every cook has a favorite casserole recipe. This will be equally tasty with chicken if your hunting skills come up short.

Baked Ruffed Grouse

breast fillets from 4–6 grouse or pheasants
½ cup flour
1 teaspoon salt
1 teaspoon paprika
1 teaspoon seasoned salt
¼ cup butter
2 teaspoons cornstarch
1½ cups half & half, divided
1 teaspoon grated lemon zest
1 tablespoon lemon juice
¼ cup sherry
½ cup Swiss cheese, shredded

Combine flour, salt, paprika and seasoned salt. Dredge meat and lightly brown in butter in large frying pan over medium heat. Remove meat from pan and place in a 9x13 baking dish. Mix cornstarch with ½ cup of the half & half and stir into the pan drippings. Cook over low heat and slowly stir in remaining half & half, lemon zest, lemon juice and sherry. Cook about 10 minutes or until mixture thickens. Pour the mixture over the meat. Cover and bake at 350° for 35 minutes, uncover and sprinkle on cheese, bake an additional 5 minutes.

After a golden day in the forest, this superb presentation of your elusive quarry will guarantee total satisfaction.

Campfire Grouse

FOR EACH PERSON
1 bird
1½ tablespoons butter
½ teaspoon salt
¼ teaspoon black pepper

Split birds down the middle, rub well with butter, salt and pepper. Broil over glowing coals for about 8 minutes per side or until done to your taste. Serve with roast onions made by cross-slicing a medium onion halfway through, dab on 1 teaspoon butter and a little seasoned salt, roll in aluminum foil and toss in the coals for 6–8 minutes.

Coal-baked potatoes and sweet corn should also accompany this meal.

When you're the camp cook and the gunning has been good, this simple, tasty recipe will forge bonds that could last forever.

Grouse Hash

1 pint canned grouse, pheasant or dove
4 tablespoons vegetable oil
6–8 medium potatoes, peeled and sliced
1 medium onion, diced
1 sweet red pepper, diced
1 green pepper, diced
1 can cream of chicken soup
½ cup milk
1 teaspoon salt
½ teaspoon black pepper
½ teaspoon seasoned salt

In a large frying pan heat oil and fry potatoes, adding onion and peppers when potatoes are browned. Continue frying for another 5–6 minutes or until onion and peppers are tender. In medium saucepan combine soup, milk, spices and meat. Combine with the potatoes and serve hot.

Serves well with fried eggs and toast for a great camp breakfast.

This is my favorite deer camp breakfast.

Quail & Wild Rice

8 quail (about 2 lbs.)
4 strips bacon
1 cup shredded carrots
½ cup sliced green onion
½ cup minced fresh parsley
2½ cups chicken broth
½ cup brown rice
½ cup wild rice
½ teaspoon salt
¼ teaspoon lemon pepper

In large skillet or Dutch oven fry bacon over medium heat until partially done. Remove bacon and brown the quail in the drippings. Remove and keep warm. Sauté carrots, onion, and parsley in drippings until tender. Drain excess grease. Add broth, rice, salt, and seasonings. Bring to a boil. Place birds over rice, put a half bacon strip over each bird. Reduce heat, cover and simmer for 35–45 minutes or until rice is tender. Serve with hot bread. Serves 4.

Touched with a fine wine, memories of hunts past will be shared and treasured.

Dove & Baked Bean Stew

breast fillets from 10 doves
4 slices thick bacon
1 medium onion, chopped
1 green bell pepper, chopped
2 cloves garlic, minced
2 15-oz. cans baked beans
1 15-oz. can garbanzo beans
1 15-oz. can diced tomatoes
½ teaspoon dried sage
½ teaspoon ground cumin
½ teaspoon salt
¼ teaspoon black pepper

Cut bacon into small chunks and fry in Dutch oven over medium-high heat. Add meat, onion, green pepper and garlic and cook 4–5 minutes. Add beans, tomatoes, herbs and seasonings. Heat to a slow bubbling boil. Reduce heat and simmer uncovered for 20 minutes. Serve with hot French bread.

Set on the camp stove with a ready ladle, this pot will empty faster than a dove in flight.

Dove Appetizers

dove breasts
Italian dressing
pepperjack cheese, cut into small pieces
bacon, thinly sliced

Fillet dove breasts and marinate in Italian dressing for 1 hour. Make a slit in each breast large enough to insert a piece of cheese. Wrap with one-third of a slice of bacon and secure with toothpick. Grill over low heat using a grill plate, turning frequently to prevent burning and sticking. When the bacon is browned the tidbit is ready to eat. Serve hot off the grill.

Doesn't matter how many doves you have. They will all disappear once they are cooked.

Dove Casserole

breast fillets from 8–12 doves
½ cup flour
½ teaspoon seasoned salt
¼ teaspoon black pepper
4 tablespoons butter
1 small can mushrooms, sliced
1 stalk celery, minced
1 tablespoon orange zest
2 cups dry white wine

Mix flour, seasoned salt and pepper. Dredge breast fillets. Melt butter over medium heat in large frying pan and sauté breasts until golden brown. Place breast fillets in a casserole large enough to allow a single layer.

Sprinkle mushrooms, celery and orange zest over fillets, pour in wine. Cover and bake at 325° for 30 minutes or until tender.

Serve with steamed carrots and broccoli.

A tantalizing feast to welcome the first gunning of the season.

Dove Creole

8–12 dove breast fillets
½ teaspoon salt
¼ teaspoon pepper
½ teaspoon Cajun-Creole seasoning
1 can stewed tomatoes
3 cloves garlic, crushed
1 large onion, chopped
1 stalk celery, chopped
1 green bell pepper, chopped
1 can mushrooms
1 hot red pepper, chopped

Place all ingredients in slow cooker or crock pot. Cover and cook on high setting for 5–6 hours. Serve with potatoes or rice.

When the crock pot does all the work, the camp cook has time to enjoy a lighter moment with his buddies.

Dove Stroganoff

breast fillets from 10–15 doves
2 tablespoons butter
3 tablespoons flour
½ teaspoon black pepper
1 large onion, minced
1 small can of mushrooms
1 clove garlic, minced
2 cups water
2 beef bouillon cubes (preferably Knorr)
2 tablespoons ketchup
1 teaspoon salt
1 cup sour cream
1 package noodles, prepared following directions
on package

Melt butter over medium-high heat in a heavy skillet. Dredge the dove breasts in flour and pepper and brown lightly. Remove from the pan. Add onion, mushrooms and garlic and sauté until tender. Return the meat to the skillet, add water, bouillon, ketchup and salt. Cover and simmer for 20 minutes. Blend the remaining flour and pepper with some of the broth and stir into the skillet. Heat to boiling. Slow boil for one minute, stirring constantly, then reduce heat and stir in sour cream. Serve over hot noodles with warm crusty bread.

A delightful way to prepare this tiny quarry.

Canned Pheasant Pâté

1 pint canned pheasant, drained
4 oz. cream cheese
½ cup light sour cream
1 small jalapeno pepper, minced
1 tablespoon minced onion
¼ teaspoon salt
¼ teaspoon Worcestershire sauce
dash Cajun seasoning

In a medium bowl, combine cream cheese and sour cream with peppers, onion and seasonings. Cut up or grind pheasant if necessary and blend with cheese mixture. Cover and refrigerate for 2–4 hours before serving. Serve with garlic toast or crackers.

Any gathering of like-minded souls will welcome and enjoy this tasty treat.

Creamy White Pheasant Chili

3–4 pheasant breasts cut into ½" cubes
4 tablespoons flour
3 tablespoons vegetable oil
1 medium onion, chopped
3 large cloves garlic, minced
1 stalk celery, chopped
2 15½-oz. cans Great Northern Beans, rinsed and drained
2 14½-oz. cans chicken broth
2 4-oz. cans green chilies
¼ teaspoon salt
½ teaspoon ground cumin
½ teaspoon pepper
½ teaspoon cayenne pepper or Cajun seasoning
1 cup sour cream
½ cup heavy whipping cream

Dredge the meat in flour and lightly brown in oil in a large skillet over medium-high heat. Remove meat chunks from pan and lightly sauté onion, garlic and celery. Return the pheasant chunks to the skillet and add beans, chicken broth, chilies, salt, cumin, pepper and cayenne. Bring to a boil. Reduce heat and simmer uncovered for 30 minutes. Remove from heat and stir in sour cream and heavy whipping cream and serve immediately. Pheasant may be substituted with chicken, quail or partridge.

Outstanding, a favorite among the shooters after a couple of rounds of winter five-stand.

Pheasant & Wild Rice Salad

WILD RICE
3½ cups water
½ teaspoon salt
1 chicken bouillon cube
1 cup wild rice, rinsed

Bring water to boil. Add salt, bouillon and rice, then cover and reduce heat to simmer. Cook approximately 1 hour or until rice is tender. Drain excess water; cool.

PHEASANT MIX
1 pheasant, deboned, cut into bite-sized chunks
1 cup broccoli buds
1 cup chopped celery
½ cup sliced baby carrots
½ cup sliced green onion
½ cup chopped red pepper

Sauté meat in skillet over medium heat, turning occasionally, for 6–8 minutes. Remove from heat. Cool, then mix with vegetables.

DRESSING
1 cup mayonnaise
1 tablespoon mustard
1 tablespoon lemon juice
2 tablespoons milk
¼ teaspoon dill weed
¼ teaspoon white pepper
dash of Cajun seasoning
½ teaspoon seasoned salt

Blend all dressing ingredients with rice and pheasant mixture in large bowl and refrigerate at least 3–4 hours before serving. Time improves this dish.

Turkey or even chicken can also be used.

Pheasant Casserole Simmered in Wine

2 pheasants (breast halves and thighs)
salt and pepper
1 cup pancake mix
¼ cup olive oil
1 large onion, sliced
2 cloves garlic, mashed
1 sweet red pepper, sliced
1 cup water
2 beef bouillon cubes
2 cups wine (either red or white)
3 tablespoons tomato paste

Sprinkle salt and pepper on the pheasant pieces and dredge in the pancake mix. Heat the olive oil in a heavy frying pan or skillet and brown the meat. Remove the pheasant and lightly sauté the onion, garlic and pepper. Drain any excess oil from the pan. Return the pheasant to the pan, add water, bouillon and wine and stir in the tomato paste. Cover and simmer, stirring occasionally, for 30–40 minutes or until meat is tender. Serve over a bed of hot noodles and enjoy.

Simple to prepare, elegant to present, always enjoyed.

Pheasant Dijon

1 pheasant, cut into serving pieces
4 tablespoons butter
1 cup water
1 cup white wine
¼ teaspoon dried tarragon
½ teaspoon seasoned salt
¼ teaspoon black pepper
2 egg yolks
2 tablespoons sour cream
2 tablespoons Dijon-style mustard
paprika

Melt butter in heavy frying pan or skillet over medium-high heat. Add pheasant, brown well. Add water, wine, tarragon, seasoned salt and pepper; bring to a boil. Reduce heat, cover and simmer for 30 minutes or until meat is fork tender. Transfer meat to a serving dish and keep warm.

In a small bowl add several tablespoons of the liquid from the pan, egg yolks, sour cream and mustard and blend well. Stir into remaining juices in the pan, stirring constantly over medium-low heat; do not boil. Pour sauce over pheasant and sprinkle with paprika. Serve with wild rice.

The magic of mustard gives flavor and character to this dish.

Pheasant Pasta

1 pheasant breast cut into bite-sized pieces
8 oz. fettuccini or other pasta
1 tablespoon olive oil
1 clove garlic, crushed
1 cup chopped green onion
1 cup chopped broccoli florets
½ cup chopped sweet red pepper
½ cup chopped celery
½ cup chopped carrots

SAUCE
2 tablespoons butter
2 tablespoons flour
2 cups milk
2 chicken bouillon cubes
½ teaspoon salt
¼ teaspoon pepper
dash of cayenne pepper or Cajun seasoning

Prepare pasta using directions on package and drain. In large skillet over medium heat sauté pheasant chunks in oil and garlic 3–4 minutes. Add remaining veggies and stir fry for an additional 6–8 minutes.

To make sauce, melt butter in medium saucepan, stir in flour, add milk and bring to low boil. Reduce heat, add bouillon and seasoning and simmer 6–8 minutes, stirring frequently. Add to stir fry, blend with pasta and enjoy.

Serve with a good wine and your guests will rave.

Pheasant Pâté

2–3 pheasant breasts
2 cups chicken broth
6 green onions, minced
1 tablespoon minced red pepper
1 tablespoon minced yellow pepper
1 tablespoon minced celery
1 teaspoon minced garlic
2 cups real mayonnaise
1 cup sour cream
1 tablespoon Knorr Vegetable Soup and Dip Mix
salt and pepper

In a medium kettle simmer the meat in chicken broth until fork tender, approximately 20 minutes. Remove from heat, drain and let cool.

Prepare the onions, peppers, celery and garlic and put in large bowl. Add mayo, sour cream and soup mix and blend. Add salt and pepper to taste.

Run the pheasant meat through a food processor and add to the mixture. Blend and transfer to a plastic container, seal and refrigerate at least 4 hours. Serve with garlic toast, toasted bagels or crackers.

I served this pâté on a toasted onion bagel for breakfast when Ted Nugent was my guest. He, like everyone else who's tried it, loved it.

Pheasant Pesto

2 pheasant breasts, skinned and boneless
2 tablespoons flour
½ teaspoon salt
¼ teaspoon black pepper
⅛ teaspoon garlic powder
3 tablespoons olive oil
1 medium onion, chopped
1 stalk celery, chopped
1 sweet red pepper, chopped
1 cup chopped carrot
3 cups milk
1 package Knorr Pesto Sauce mix
1 16-oz. box angel hair pasta
fresh Parmesan cheese, grated

Cut meat into bite-sized pieces. Mix flour, salt, pepper and garlic powder. Dredge meat in flour mixture. In a large skillet over medium-high heat, brown meat on both sides in olive oil. Add vegetables and stir fry for approximately 5 minutes.

Heat milk in a medium saucepan over medium-high heat and whisk or stir in pesto sauce mix. Bring to boil, stirring frequently. Reduce heat to simmer. Add pheasant and vegetables and cook for an additional 20 minutes. Prepare pasta following package directions. Toss cooked and drained pasta with sauce. Serve with grated Parmesan cheese and garlic toast.

This unique variation of pheasant with pasta offers yet another dimension to your kitchen creations.

Pheasant Poppers

breast meat from 2–3 pheasants
2 sweet red bell peppers
1 cup barbecue sauce
1 lb. bacon, thinly sliced
salt and pepper

Thinly slice the pheasant breasts across the grain (you will end up with a piece approximately 1½" x 2½" x ¼"). Cut the red peppers into strips approximately ½" wide and 1½" long. Lightly salt and pepper the pheasant pieces and dip in barbecue sauce. Place half a strip of bacon on cutting board, place pheasant meat on the bacon and top with the red pepper. Roll the bacon and pheasant around the pepper and secure with a toothpick, making sure to skewer the pepper. Place on a grill plate over hot coals and grill 4–5 minutes on each side. These delicate little tidbits must be tended at the grill to keep them from burning. When the bacon is browned, baste with remaining sauce and serve.

A tasty creation loved by all.

Pheasant Soup

carcasses from 2 pheasants
4 quarts water
1 teaspoon salt
1 stalk celery, minced
2 carrots, minced
4–6 chicken bouillon cubes
1 cup rice, uncooked

EGG DROPS
4 eggs
1½ cups flour
¼ teaspoon baking powder
½ teaspoon salt
1 teaspoon parsley flakes

Clean and rinse pheasants, place in soup pot with water and salt. Cover and boil over medium heat for 30 minutes. Remove from heat, skim froth from broth, clean meat from bones. Return meat to the pot and add celery, carrots, bouillon and rice. Cover and simmer 30–45 minutes.

To make egg drops, beat eggs until frothy, add other ingredients and mix well. Batter should be stiff; add more flour if necessary. Drop by spoonfuls in broth. Simmer 10–12 minutes.

Many of the recipes for pheasant call for only the breast meat, and to waste the rest of the carcass is practically unthinkable. Therefore, save those remaining parts and use them to make a delicate broth from which you can create your best soup ever.

Pheasant Stuffing Casserole

1 pheasant, cut into bite-sized pieces
1 stick butter
2 cups chopped onion
1 cup chopped celery
½ cup chopped red pepper
1 cup sliced mushrooms
½ cup chopped carrots
1 8-oz. package seasoned croutons
2 cups cooked wild rice
½ teaspoon black pepper
½ teaspoon salt
1 tablespoon parsley flakes
2 14-oz. cans chicken broth

Melt butter in large nonstick skillet over medium heat. Add pheasant meat and sauté approximately 5 minutes. Remove meat, set aside. Add onion, celery, red pepper, mushrooms and carrots and sauté 6–8 minutes.

In large bowl combine croutons, cooked wild rice, meat, vegetables and seasonings. Place in greased roaster or large glass baking dish, drizzle broth over stuffing and cover. Bake for 20 minutes at 325°. Remove cover and bake an additional 10 minutes.

Introduce your family to the goodness of wild fowl with this tempting creation, which is sure to please.

Pheasant Tenders

breast meat from 4–6 pheasants
4–6 teaspoons hot sauce
1 cup pancake mix
enough oil to deep fry

Cut the pheasant breasts into finger-sized strips. Place in bowl or plastic container and add hot sauce. Cover and refrigerate for several hours. Dredge in pancake mix and deep fry at 375° until golden; drain on paper towel or brown paper and enjoy.

When the gunning is fast and limits come easy, time is on your side to prepare these tender tidbits for the hunting crew. Seems there are never enough.

Pheasant with Mushroom & Wine Sauce

breast halves from 2 pheasants
1 can cream of mushroom soup
1 teaspoon dried parsley
¼ cup white wine
1 clove garlic, crushed
½ cup skim milk
1 teaspoon onion soup mix
½ lb. fresh mushrooms, sliced
½ teaspoon salt
¼ teaspoon black pepper

Place all ingredients in a crock pot or slow cooker and mix well. Submerge pheasant breasts in the liquid. Cover and cook on low setting for 6 hours. Serve with wild rice and hot bread.

Prepared in a crock pot, your supper will be ready when you return from that late-afternoon hunt.

Roast Pheasant Provincial

1 whole pheasant, cleaned and rinsed
1 clove garlic, minced
3 tablespoons olive oil
1 tablespoon hot and spicy mustard
¼ teaspoon thyme
½ teaspoon seasoned salt
3 cups cooked wild rice
½ cup minced celery
½ cup chopped mushrooms
¼ cup minced onion
¼ cup minced sweet red pepper

Combine garlic, oil, mustard and seasonings. Coat bird inside and out. In a medium bowl combine the cooked rice, celery, mushrooms, onion and red pepper and fill the cavity of the bird. Wrap in aluminum foil and bake in a shallow pan at 375° for 1 hour and 15 minutes.

Enjoy the feast.

Skillet Pheasant with Wild Rice

1 breast of pheasant, meat removed from the bone
1 tablespoon olive oil
2 tablespoons flour
1 medium onion, chopped
1 red pepper, chopped
1 yellow pepper, chopped
2 cups broccoli florets
2 cups cauliflower florets
½ cup chicken broth
2 cups cooked wild rice
1 cup shredded cojack or other mild cheese
choice of seasonings (I use a black pepper-based seasoning that works very well, but season to your taste.)

Start by preparing the wild rice according to directions on package. It generally takes a full hour to cook tender.

Heat the oil in a large frying pan or skillet over medium-high heat. Dredge the pheasant meat in flour and brown on both sides.

Remove the meat from the pan, add onion and peppers and sauté until tender. Add broccoli and cauliflower, stir fry for about 2–3 minutes. Add chicken broth, cover and steam for 3–4 minutes or until veggies are tender crisp. Mix in the cooked wild rice. Return the pheasant to the pan, season to taste, sprinkle with the cheese, cover and remove from heat. When the cheese has melted, serve at once. This recipe would lend itself well to creating individual servings in cast iron or ceramic dishes.

You must try this dish. Henceforth you will fix and serve it at least once every season.

Stuffed Pheasant Breasts

4 pheasant breast halves, skinless and boneless
1 tablespoon butter
1 cup finely diced acorn squash
1 red bell pepper, diced
1 small onion, finely diced
1 stalk celery, chopped
salt and pepper to taste
1 cup all-purpose flour for dredging
2 oz. shredded cheddar cheese

Preheat oven to 350°. Lightly grease a 9x13 baking dish. In a medium skillet, melt butter. Add the squash, red bell pepper, onion and celery. Sauté until slightly tender. Season to taste with salt and pepper. Remove from heat. Slice pheasant breasts on the side about ¾ of the way through to make a pocket. Stuff mixture evenly into each slit breast until full. Pin with toothpick to hold. Dredge each breast in flour to coat and brown in skillet. Place browned pheasant breasts in the prepared baking dish, cover and bake in the preheated oven for about 25 minutes or until meat is cooked through and juices run clear. Sprinkle with cheese and serve.

When there's just the two of you, this special dinner will set the mood for a truly enchanted evening.

Fried Breast of Wild Turkey

1 turkey breast, boned
2 eggs
¼ cup milk
1 tablespoon white wine
¼ teaspoon seasoned salt
4 tablespoons vegetable oil
2 tablespoons butter
1 package saltine crackers, finely crushed

Cut turkey into strips. In small bowl beat eggs, milk, wine and salt. Heat oil and butter in a large skillet over medium-high heat. Dip each turkey strip in egg mixture, dredge and coat in crushed crackers. Fry until golden brown.

The old gobbler will once again strut through your thoughts as you devour these tasty turkey fingers.

Grilled Turkey Rolls

½ turkey breast, deboned
1 bottle Jack Daniels #7 BBQ Sauce
1 lb. bacon, thinly sliced

Cut the breast meat across the grain into thin strips. Dip each piece of turkey meat into the sauce, place it on half a strip of bacon, then roll together and secure with a toothpick. Use a greased grill plate and place about 4" above the coals on a hot grill. Tend carefully and turn frequently to prevent burning. Baste with the remaining barbecue sauce in the final minutes on the grill.

A little labor intensive if you are cooking for a crowd, but a sure pleaser in any setting.

Smoked Turkey Salad

3 cups smoked turkey, cut into bite-sized pieces
4 hard-boiled eggs, chopped
1 cup chopped red onion
½ cup chopped celery
1 jalapeno pepper, chopped
1½ cups mayonnaise
1 teaspoon Dijon-style mustard
½ teaspoon white pepper
½ teaspoon black pepper
½ teaspoon salt

In large bowl, combine turkey, eggs, onion, celery and jalapeno pepper. In separate bowl blend the mayonnaise with the remaining ingredients. Add the mayonnaise mixture to the turkey mixture and blend thoroughly. Refrigerate at least 2 hours to enhance flavors. Serve on croissants or toasted English muffins. Serves 6–8.

The versatile wild turkey is fun to hunt and fun to eat. This recipe breaks with traditional cooking and offers a change of menu.

Turkey Chili

4 cups turkey meat, cooked and chopped
3 tablespoons butter
1 large onion, chopped
2 cups chopped celery
1 cup chopped carrots
½ cup chopped red pepper
1 large can chicken broth
1 can white beans, drained and rinsed
1 14.5-oz. can diced tomatoes
1 teaspoon cumin
½ teaspoon coriander
½ teaspoon chili powder
½ teaspoon black pepper
½ teaspoon tabasco sauce

In large pot melt butter over medium-high heat. Add onion, celery, carrots and red pepper. Cook, stirring occasionally, until vegetables are softened, about 8–10 minutes. Add turkey, then stir in broth, beans, tomatoes and seasonings. Bring to slow boil, reduce heat and simmer 30–45 minutes.

This crowd pleaser will always be welcome after a cold day in the outdoors.

Wild Turkey & Dumpling Stew

2 lbs. turkey breast, cut into 1" cubes
4 lean bacon strips, diced
2 cups chopped baby carrots
2 cups chopped celery
1 medium onion, chopped
½ cup chopped sweet red pepper
4 cups water
6 chicken bouillon cubes
¼ teaspoon crushed dried rosemary
½ teaspoon salt
¼ teaspoon black pepper
2 tablespoons flour

DUMPLINGS
4 eggs, beaten
1½ cups flour
¼ teaspoon baking powder
½ teaspoon seasoned salt

In a Dutch oven or large soup kettle, fry bacon until crisp. Remove bacon and brown the turkey pieces in the bacon drippings. Use a slotted spoon to remove the meat from the kettle, drain and discard the bacon drippings. Return turkey to the kettle. Add carrots, celery, onion, red pepper, water, bouillon and rosemary. Bring to boil, reduce heat. Cover and simmer for 30 minutes or until veggies are tender. Add bacon. In a closed container combine salt, pepper and flour with ¼ cup of the liquid broth and stir or shake until smooth. Stir into the turkey mixture and simmer. Continue stirring for about 2 minutes as mixture thickens.

Combine all dumpling ingredients in a bowl and stir until soft dough forms. Drop by spoonfuls in stew. Cover and cook an additional 10–12 minutes.

One of my all-time favorites; nothing else needs to be said.

Wild Turkey Pâté

1 pint canned turkey meat
1 stick butter
¼ cup cream
1 tablespoon hot & spicy mustard
1 clove garlic, minced
1 small onion, minced
½ teaspoon nutmeg
1 oz. brandy

Place all ingredients in a food processor and run until smooth. Transfer to a serving dish, cover and refrigerate for 6 hours. Serve with crackers or garlic toast.

When you are limited to one bird per season, some thought must be given to your favorite recipes. This one should always be on your list.

Waterfowl Gumbo

meat from 1–2 geese or large ducks, boned and cubed
4 quarts water
4 chicken bouillon cubes
2 chicken breasts, cubed
1 cup olive oil
1 cup flour
2 large onions, chopped
1 green pepper, chopped
1 sweet red pepper, chopped
1 ring smoked venison country-style sausage
2 tablespoon Cajun-Creole seasoning
1 tablespoon tabasco sauce
1 teaspoon black pepper
1 16-oz. can stewed tomatoes
1 lb. frozen okra, chopped
1 lb. shrimp, cleaned and deveined
1 teaspoon gumbo filé

In a large soup pot over medium-high heat boil water and bouillon and add meat from both wild fowl and chicken. (If the meat has not been removed from the bone, cook until meat falls from the bone then remove bones from the liquid and cut the meat into bite-sized pieces.)

In a large skillet, heat oil, stir in the flour and cook until the roux thickens and turns brown. Add onions and pepper; stir and cook for a few minutes. Add sausage, reduce heat and cook for an additional 10 minutes, stirring frequently. Combine the contents of the skillet with the meat and liquid in the soup pot. Add seasoning, tabasco sauce and pepper and bring to a low boil. Reduce heat and cook for approximately 2 hours. Add stewed tomatoes, okra and shrimp and simmer for an additional hour or so. Add filé several minutes before serving.

Serve over a bed of steaming rice with hot crusty bread.

Waterfowl Hot Dish

2 lbs. duck or goose meat, cubed
4 cups water
1 cup wild rice, uncooked
1 teaspoon salt
4 tablespoons butter
2 cloves garlic, minced
1 large onion, chopped
2 stalks celery, chopped
1 green bell pepper, chopped
1 can cream of chicken soup
1 can cream of mushroom soup
1 cup milk
½ teaspoon salt
¼ teaspoon pepper
1 can "jumbo" ready-to-bake buttermilk biscuits

In a medium saucepan cook the rice in 4 cups of water and 1 teaspoon salt for 30–40 minutes or until kernels pop. Melt butter in large frying pan and gently brown the meat with garlic. Drain off any fat, mix meat with rice and veggies and place in large ovenproof baking dish. Mix soups with milk; add salt and pepper and pour over meat and rice mixture. Bake at 350° for 50 minutes. Separate biscuits and arrange on top of the hotdish. Return to oven and bake an additional 15 minutes or until biscuits are golden brown.

I believe time shared in a duck blind is not subtracted from your life.

Waterfowl Stew

breast meat from 2 small geese, cut into bite-sized pieces
¼ cup olive or vegetable oil
1 ring smoked venison country-style sausage, sliced
1 large onion, chopped
2 stalks celery, chopped
1 sweet red pepper, chopped
½ lb. fresh mushrooms
1 can cream of mushroom soup
1 cup white wine
2 chicken bouillon cubes
½ teaspoon salt
½ teaspoon black pepper
1 lb. shrimp, cleaned and deveined

Heat oil in a large frying pan or skillet and sauté both the goose and venison sausage until lightly browned, about 6–8 minutes. Remove meat from the skillet; add onion, celery, red pepper and mushrooms and sauté 3–4 minutes. Drain excess oil from the pan. Return meat to the skillet, add soup, wine, bouillon, salt and pepper. Simmer 30–40 minutes. Add shrimp and cook an additional 5 minutes. Serve over a bed of steaming wild rice or cooked pasta.

Hearty enough for any appetite after a long day in the marsh.

Crock Pot Duck

2 ducks, quartered
4 tablespoons butter
1 onion, chopped
1 stalk celery, chopped
½ cup orange juice
½ teaspoon seasoned salt
1 teaspoon hot & spicy mustard
1 tablespoon orange zest
½ cup heavy red or port wine

Melt butter over medium heat in a medium saucepan. Add onion and celery; sauté gently. Add orange juice, seasoned salt, mustard, orange zest and wine. Place duck pieces in a crock pot or slow cooker. Pour sauce over the meat, cook on low heat for approximately 8 hours.

The best part of life is spent hunting and fishing; the rest is wasted.

Duck Breast with Chokecherry Sauce

2 mallard breast fillets
¼ cup flour
½ teaspoon seasoned salt
¼ teaspoon black pepper
2 tablespoons butter
4 tablespoons vermouth
2 tablespoons chokecherry jelly

Use meat mallet to flatten each breast fillet to ¼" thick. Mix flour, seasoned salt and pepper. In a heavy frying pan, melt butter. Dredge the meat in the flour mixture and brown on each side, then transfer the meat to a heated platter. Add vermouth and jelly to the pan and blend with cooking juices to make sauce. Pour sauce over fillets and serve with rice.

Cooked on a camp stove or in the kitchen, you'll be satisfied with this dish. Be sure not to overcook the meat.

Duck Breast with Mushroom Sauce

breast fillets from 2 large ducks
½ cup flour
1 teaspoon seasoned salt
¼ teaspoon black pepper
2 tablespoons corn oil
8 oz. fresh mushrooms, sliced
1 small onion, minced
2 cans cream of mushroom soup
⅓ cup milk
¼ cup white wine

In a shallow bowl, mix flour, seasoned salt and pepper. Dredge meat to coat. Heat oil in a large frying pan over medium-high heat and brown the breasts. Remove from pan. Add mushrooms and onion and sauté for approximately 6 minutes or until onion is transparent. Add mushroom soup, milk and wine. Stir to blend. Add meat and simmer for an additional 15 minutes. Serve over rice, potatoes or noodles.

A cautionary word to the young: Don't brag up the camp cook's skills when you get home. Let Mom think you were really roughing it.

Smoked Duck Hash

2 smoked breast fillets from duck or goose, diced
3 tablespoons olive oil
6 medium potatoes, unpeeled and shredded
1 onion, minced
half of a sweet red pepper, minced
½ cup shredded carrots
½ teaspoon salt
¼ teaspoon black pepper
1 tablespoon chopped fresh thyme
½ cup light sour cream
1 teaspoon ground horseradish

Heat oil in a large skillet over medium-high heat and fry the potatoes until lightly browned. Add onion, meat, red pepper, carrots, salt, pepper and thyme and fry until potatoes are golden brown, turning as needed.

In a small bowl combine the sour cream and horseradish and serve on the side of the Smoked Duck Hash.

Serve as a one-pot meal or as a side dish to thick, charbroiled venison steaks.

Easy Oven Goose Jerky

breast fillets from 2–4 geese
½ cup soy sauce
1 cup teriyaki sauce
1 shot bourbon
1 cup red wine
1 tablespoon Worcestershire sauce
1 teaspoon freshly ground black pepper
2 teaspoons rosemary
½ teaspoon onion powder

Mix all of the ingredients except goose fillets in a gallon-size sealable plastic bag. Slice the breast meat with the grain in strips ¼" thick. Place the sliced meat in the bag and refrigerate overnight.

Spray the oven rack with cooking spray and place aluminum foil on the bottom of the oven. Drape the meat strips over the oven rack and bake at 165–175° for approximately 6 hours. To let the moisture escape from the oven, prop the door open several inches. Monitor periodically so the meat doesn't get overcooked. The objective is to dry the meat to a flexible consistency so it will bend but not be so dry it breaks.

In an attempt to control the burgeoning snow goose population and restore Arctic habitat, limits have been relaxed. Use this recipe to help consume your harvest.

Goose with Chokecherry Sauce

breast fillets from 1 giant Canada goose
1 medium onion, chopped
1 clove of garlic
1 beef bouillon cube
1 cup water
½ cup chokecherry jelly
½ cup hot & spicy mustard

In a crock pot or slow cooker combine onion, garlic, bouillon, water and meat. Cover and cook on high heat for 6 hours. Remove meat from crock pot and set aside until cool enough to handle, then cut into ½" cubes. Combine jelly and mustard with the liquid remaining in the crock pot and mix well. Return the cubed meat to the crock pot and simmer on low heat for an additional 1–2 hours.

Serve as an appetizer.

For everything there is a season. I like hunting season the best.

Grilled Goose Breast with Peppers

breast fillets from 2–4 snow geese
½ cup olive oil
¼ cup soy sauce
1 oz. Jack Daniels Bourbon
6 cloves garlic, minced
1 jar pickled jalapeno peppers
8 slices bacon

In each breast fillet, cut several slits with a sharp knife. Combine the olive oil, soy sauce, bourbon and garlic. Layer the meat in a shallow plastic container. Pour the liquid mixture over the meat and refrigerate for several hours, turning at least once. Remove the fillets from marinade, insert a slice of jalapeno pepper into each of the slits, wrap each breast with bacon and secure with toothpicks. Grill on a grill plate approximately 4" over the hot coals for 5–6 minutes per side, taking care not to overcook. Generally, when the bacon is browned the meat on the inside will be perfect.

These tender bacon wraps are delicious and will elevate your status as camp cook to new levels.

Steam-Roasted Canada Goose

1 large goose, plucked, dressed and cleaned
juice from 1 fresh lemon
salt

STUFFING
4 tablespoons butter
2 medium onions, minced
3 stalks celery, minced
10 fresh mushrooms, sliced
1 teaspoon salt
3 cups croutons
½ teaspoon pepper
¼ teaspoon allspice
½ cup port wine

Clean all loose fat from inside the bird. Cut off the wing tips at elbow, the neck close to body, and the tail. With fork or sharp knife prick skin at the base of each wing, the backs of the legs and where thigh meets back to prevent accumulation of melted fat. Rub bird inside and out with lemon juice and lightly salt the cavity. Place on rack in roaster pan breast side up. Add 1" of water to the pan, place on top of stove, bring to boil, reduce heat, cover and steam for 1 hour. Add more water if necessary; do not burn dry.

To make the stuffing, melt butter in heavy frying pan over medium heat, lightly sauté onion and celery, then add mushrooms. Stir in croutons and seasonings. Pour wine over top and mix gently, then remove from heat.

Preheat oven to 325°. Remove goose from roaster and let cool 15–20 minutes. Discard liquid from the bottom of the pan. Loosely fill the cavity of the goose with stuffing; use skewers and string to close opening, replace goose on rack in roasting pan. Add 2 cups water and roast covered 2–3 hours, depending on size of bird. After 1½ hours baste bird every 15 minutes and remove cover for the final 30 minutes to brown. Make gravy from the pan drippings, and let your creativity flow as you prepare the rest of the meal to complement this noble bird.

Stuffed Breast of Goose

6–8 goose breast fillets
4 bacon slices, diced
1 stalk celery, minced
1 medium onion, minced
1 sweet red pepper, minced
1 green pepper, minced
1 jalapeno pepper, minced
¼ cup barbecue sauce
½ cup shredded cheddar cheese
½ cup shredded mozzarella cheese

Fry bacon over medium-high heat until golden, then add veggies and sauté briefly, about 1–2 minutes. Stir in barbecue sauce and cook an additional 2–3 minutes. Remove from heat and allow to cool. When mixture is cool, blend in the cheese. Make a pocket in each breast fillet by slicing along one side. Stuff each pocket with veggie and cheese mixture and seal with a toothpick. Grill over hot coals for 6–8 minutes on the first side, and approximately 4 minutes on the second side. Serve medium rare; do not overcook.

Cook this recipe for those who express a dislike for the flavor of wild ducks and geese; one bite and watch the attitude change.

Fish

A Few Helpful Hints about Fish

Given today's technology and equipment, anglers are catching and bringing home more fish than our forefathers ever dreamed about. At any time our freezers are likely to hold white bass, smallmouth bass, perch, crappies, catfish, Northern pike, any variety of trout, salmon and, of course, our premiere fish—the walleye. Our objective here is to show and describe the versatility of fish, tasty cooking options for different fish and the creative characteristics in each of us. Each species has its own special characteristics. Some fish are fatty and some are lean. Some grow to huge size while others are a trophy if they reach a pound. Fishing offers variety, and given the versatility of fish, we need to be equally versatile and creative in the preparation of our catch. Many factors will influence the taste and quality long before it gets to our table.

Care at the Lake or Stream: Fish are very perishable and should be kept alive or put on ice when they are pulled from the water. Fish kept on a stringer and dragged through water with a surface temperature of 70 plus degrees and the hot sun beating down will spoil rapidly. Fish caught on extended trips should be field dressed and packed in crushed ice with rock salt (1 lb. of salt per 20 lbs. of ice). Also, drain the cooler often so the fish does not lie in water.

Cleaning: Quality fish destined for your table should be cleaned as soon as reasonably possible. Large fish that are to be steaked should be field dressed (remove guts and gills) as soon as possible. Scale fish that are to be cooked with the skin on. Most fish can be readily filleted with a sharp knife. Remove the Y bones and cut off the thin strip of belly meat. This is generally fatty, tastes fishy and holds any contaminants absorbed by the fish. Trim off the dark colored flesh located along the lateral line. This is also fatty and the first to spoil in or out of the freezer.

Using All of the Fish: Some flesh remains on the bones and head after filleting; don't waste it. Keep some of the backbones and heads to make a richly flavored stock for sauces, soups and chowder. Simply cover the bones with water in a saucepan, heat to boiling, then simmer for 30–40 minutes. Remove the flesh for fish cakes or salad, strain the liquid and cook down until reduced by half. Freeze in plastic containers of 1–2 cups. (Fish stock loses flavor rapidly so use within 1 month.)

Storing Fish: For the best flavor and texture, clean and cook your fish within 2 hours of catching it. Fish can be refrigerated for up to 2 days without losing much flavor. Fish not to be eaten within 24 hours should be frozen immediately. Fish to be frozen should be protected from the air, which causes freezer burn. Frost-free freezers absorb moisture, including ice; therefore, all fish to be stored in frost-free freezers should be frozen in water. The most convenient and economical method I've found to freeze fish is to use clean empty milk cartons. Simply open the tops along the seam, fill with the desired amount of fish and add water until it covers the fish. Staple the tops shut and mark the container with species and date with a permanent marker. Lean fish (e.g., pike, bass and halibut) frozen in this method should be used within 6 months. Fatty fish (e.g., trout and salmon) should be used within 3 months.

Thawing Fish: Bacteria flourishes in warm water temperatures so use caution and common sense whenever you are thawing fish. Fish thawed at room temperature should be kept out of direct sunlight and turned frequently to balance the thawing process. Drain off the water whenever possible. Refrigerate if fish is thawed prior to cooking time.

Canning Fish: Canning is an excellent alternative for preserving fish for up to one year. Canning is easy if you use a pressure cooker (which kills bacteria) and one-pint jars. Simply follow the instructions that accompany the cooker and you're in business. Recipes will call for leaving ½" of air space at the top. This, along with cleanliness and sterilizing, is the only cautionary rule. Better to have the jars not quite full than too full. Canned fish can be eaten out of the jar or used as a base for many recipes such as fish cakes, quiche, patties, pâté, etc. Once a jar is opened it should be refrigerated and consumed in 2 days.

Cooking Methods: Cooking methods will differ for fatty and lean game fish. Fatty fish should rarely be fried. However, they can be broiled, grilled over hot coals, baked, boiled, steamed, poached or smoked. All of these methods allow the fat to drain away from the fish before serving. The exceptions to this are small stream trout such as brookies, small rainbow, cutthroats, etc. These small fish have less fat and fewer calories and are frequently pan-fried, deep-fried or oven-fried.

Telling the Difference Between Fatty and Lean Fish: Generally, lean fish has white flesh, fewer calories and a mild, delicate flavor. Fatty fish has dark or pink flesh and is prone to having a strong flavor, lending itself to recipes using lemon or lime juice, wine or vinegar.

Pan Frying: Lean fish are generally excellent pan-fried. I personally think pan-fried perch fillets are the best tasting fish in the world. When pan-frying fish use a large heavy frying pan or electric country skillet to distribute the heat evenly. Use ⅛ to ¼" of canola, peanut or vegetable oil and medium or 350° heat. Do not crowd your fish when frying. Cooking time will range from 5–10 minutes. Generally if your oil is the right temperature your fish will turn a light golden color. Turn them only once, fry till golden on the other side, remove from the pan and place on a platter lined with paper towel. The towel absorbs the grease and your finished fish can be kept warm in a 175 degree oven while frying more fish.

Deep Frying Fish: Deep-frying forms a crisp, tasty golden crust around the fish and seals in moisture and flavor and seals out fat. The key to successful deep-frying is an oil temperature of 375°. Lean fish deep-fry and taste better that fatty fish. Chunks should be of uniform size. Fish pieces should be patted dry with paper towel before dipping in batter and one piece should be test fried. Batter that is too thick will fall off the fish. Batter that is too thin will not cover uniformly. Fish turn out best if both the fish and the batter are cold and the oil hot.

Baking Fish: Baking is a simple process using a shallow baking pan. However, you must be attentive and not let the fish dry out. Baking is ideal for stuffed fish or large fish, although all fish can be baked. Basting with pan juices helps prevent dryness.

Broiling Fish: Fatty fish should be selected for broiling. Trout, salmon and lake trout are ideal because of their natural oil. Baste with butter or olive oil to keep the fish moist and to enhance flavor. I generally will broil fish after boiling to improve the appearance and texture of the fish.

Poaching and Steaming Fish: This is rapidly becoming a favorite for the calorie-conscious crowd. Fish prepared by poaching is immersed in a simmering vegetable or fish broth. Cooking time is 8–10 minutes per inch of thickness and timing is not as critical as with other methods. Steaming is cooking fish on a rack above boiling wine or water. The fish is generally served with a sauce or melted butter with lemon.

Charcoal Grilling: Barbecuing fish on the grill is simple and tasty. Be sure to have a clean rack coated with oil or grease to prevent sticking. Lean fish should be basted with vegetable or olive oil and cooked with the skin side down, over the coals. Fillets or steaks without skin can be placed on foil cut roughly the same size as the fish. Fish should be basted frequently with oil or lemon butter, keeping the thickest part of the fish over the hottest coals.

Boiling Fish: Any large fish will boil nicely. This method of preparation is popular with salmon. The fish is usually scaled and cut into chunks with the skin left on. Recipes will call for adding any array of vegetables, onion, caraway seed, etc., to the water. Individual taste prevails. The water should be boiling rapidly and fish should be immersed for 10–12 minutes.

"Fishing is not about catching fish." Ya, right, try telling that to my grandkids.

Baked Fish with Rice

2 lbs. fish fillets
3 cups water
1½ cups white rice, uncooked
½ stick butter
1 onion, chopped
1 green bell pepper, chopped
1 red bell pepper, chopped
2 stalks celery, chopped
¼ cup flour
2 cups milk
1 teaspoon salt
¼ teaspoon black pepper
½ cup mild taco sauce
2 tomatoes, sliced

In a medium saucepan bring water to a boil. Add rice, reduce heat and cover. Simmer for 20 minutes. In a large skillet melt butter over medium heat; add onion, peppers and celery. Cook until tender, approximately 5 minutes. Stir in flour and add milk. Bring mixture to a boil, stirring constantly. Reduce heat to simmer, add salt, pepper and sauce. Preheat oven to 400°. Lightly grease 9x13 baking pan. Place rice in bottom of pan. Place fish over rice, cover with tomato slices and pour sauce over top. Bake at 400° for 20 minutes.

When the wind is from the south, it blows the bait right in the fish's mouth.

Fish Bake

3 lbs. boneless walleye fillets, or other white-fleshed fish such as smallmouth or striped bass
2 tablespoons butter
1 teaspoon salt
½ teaspoon black pepper
1 cup minced onion
½ cup finely chopped celery
½ cup minced red bell pepper
2 small jalapeno peppers, minced
2 cups sour cream
1 cup mayonnaise
1 tablespoon hot & spicy mustard
3 cups dry bread crumbs
½ teaspoon paprika

Preheat oven to 425°. With butter, grease a 9x13 baking dish. Cut fillets into pieces 2" wide and arrange in a single layer in pan. (Tails may be overlapped to have equal thickness.) Sprinkle fish with salt and pepper. In a medium bowl, combine the onion, celery, peppers, sour cream, mayo and mustard and blend thoroughly. Spread the mixture over the fish, then sprinkle with the bread crumbs and paprika. Bake for 25 minutes.

I didn't wake up one day and decide to become a fisherman. Rather, it took the examples of—and time shared with—my Father, uncles, cousins and friends to create this wonderful passion.

Grilled Shore Lunch

4 ½-1-lb. fillets of walleye or bass
2 tablespoons hot & spicy mustard
salt and pepper

VEGETABLE MIXTURE
2 cups shredded carrots
2 cups broccoli
1 cup chopped onion
¼ cup water
⅓ cup grated Parmesan cheese

For each fillet use a sheet of heavy-duty aluminum foil approximately 14x14". Brush both sides of the fillets with mustard. Place in center of the foil and sprinkle with salt and pepper. Combine the vegetables with the water and Parmesan cheese; place a quarter of the mixture over each fillet. Bring the 2 sides of the foil together over the fish (like a tent), leaving ample room for steam to circulate. Crimp ends also. Cook 3–4" over coals for approximately 15 minutes. Remove from heat and let rest for a few minutes. Open slowly to let steam escape. Eat right from the foil.

Regardless the intensity of the bite, there is always time to break for shore lunch and a short nap.

Tangy Fish Salad

light, flaky fish, such as bass, walleye or snapper, cooked and flaked

FOR EACH CUP OF FLAKED FISH, MIX
½ cup finely chopped or grated raw carrot
1½ cup chopped spinach
1 green onion, finely minced
½ stalk celery, diced
¼ cup bean sprouts

DRESSING
¼ cup mayonnaise
1 tablespoon tarragon vinegar
1 teaspoon lemon juice

lettuce
paprika

Combine all ingredients, mix with dressing. Shape desired portions on a bed of fresh lettuce and sprinkle with paprika.

When the coals are still hot and you need a quick lunch for the next day, simply put some fish fillets in foil and let them cook while you are enjoying the evening air. When the fish is done, put the packet in the refrigerator until you are ready to create this salad.

Grilled Bass

4–6 bass fillets
2 tablespoons olive oil
¼ cup lime juice
1 cup chardonnay wine
2 tablespoons hot & spicy mustard
2 tablespoons chili powder
2 tablespoons pepper
½ teaspoon salt

In a medium bowl combine oil, lime juice, wine, mustard and spices. Put half of the marinade in a separate bowl and reserve for basting. Place fillets in bowl and marinate for 15 minutes, turning occasionally. Remove fillets from marinade and drain. Grill or broil 4" from heat source on oiled rack. Baste with reserved marinade, cooking 4–6 minutes on each side or until it flakes easily at its thickest part.

When the spring run is on, this respite from traditional frying will give a new perspective on preparing and eating fish.

Deep-Fried Catfish & Hush Puppies

2 lbs. catfish or bullhead fillets
peanut oil
½ cup buttermilk
1 cup yellow cornmeal

Heat 3–4" of peanut oil to 375° in a deep fat fryer. Dip fish in buttermilk, then roll in cornmeal to coat. Fry a few pieces at a time for about 4 minutes or until they turn a deep golden brown. Drain on paper towel; keep warm until served.

HUSH PUPPIES
peanut oil
1 cup yellow cornmeal
⅓ cup flour
1 teaspoon sugar
1 teaspoon baking powder
⅛ teaspoon salt
⅛ teaspoon seasoned salt
1 egg
1 small onion, minced
1 8-oz. can cream-style corn
2 tablespoons buttermilk

Heat 3–4" of peanut oil to 375°. Mix dry ingredients in medium bowl, add remaining ingredients and mix lightly until combined. Drop batter into hot oil one tablespoon at a time. Fry a few at a time for 4–5 minutes or until golden brown. Drain on paper towel. Serve hot with catfish.

Fish or cut bait.

Pan-Blackened Cajun Catfish

6–8 ½-lb. fillets of catfish
3 cloves garlic, minced
3 tablespoons butter
Cajun seasoning
1 tablespoon flour
1 cup white wine

Sauté garlic in butter in a large skillet over medium heat. Liberally sprinkle both sides of each fillet with Cajun seasoning. Fry in garlic and butter for approximately 6 minutes. Turn and fry second side for 4 minutes. Remove fish from skillet and keep warm. Add flour to skillet and stir to make roux. Add wine and stir until thickened. Spoon sauce over individual portions. Enjoy!

This is how the folks Down South eat their fish. It offers a change from what we grew up with and actually tastes better than it looks.

Pan-Fried Perch Fillets

2 lbs. perch fillets
3 eggs
⅔ cup beer
½ teaspoon salt
¼ teaspoon pepper
dash Cajun seasoning
½ cup peanut or canola oil
1 package saltine crackers, finely crushed

In a medium bowl, beat eggs, then add beer and seasonings and mix thoroughly. Heat oil in frying pan or skillet to 375°. Dip fillets in egg mixture; roll in crushed crackers and place in frying pan. Fry until first side is golden brown. Turn and fry second side. Remove from pan, place on platter with paper towel to absorb oil. Serve with potato and salad.

If there truly is a Perch Heaven it must be Devils Lake, North Dakota, where the perch are fat, tasty and plentiful.

Panfish Patties

**1 dozen or so bluegills or sunfish, cleaned and with
large bones removed**
1 egg, beaten
1 cup saltine cracker crumbs
½ teaspoon salt
¼ teaspoon black pepper
4 tablespoons peanut oil

Grind fish. Place fish in a medium bowl; add egg, cracker crumbs, salt
and pepper. Blend thoroughly and form into patties. Fry in hot peanut oil in
a large skillet over high heat until golden.

I never saw an ornery kid with a fishing pole in his hand.

Ling Chowder

1½–2 lbs. ling, cut into 1" chunks
4 tablespoons butter
½ lb. bacon strips cut into 1½" pieces
2 large onions, sliced
2 large potatoes, peeled and sliced into ½" pieces
1 quart fish stock
1 pint cream
paprika
pepper

Use only the flesh above the lateral line; this can easily be skinned and cut away from the backbone.

In a large (6–8-quart) pot melt butter over medium heat. Add bacon and onion and sauté until soft. Add potatoes and mix to coat with butter. Pour in the fish stock and simmer about 15 minutes or until potatoes are almost cooked. Reduce heat and add cream. Heat until steaming (never boil), stirring frequently. Add fish and cook until done, approximately 5 minutes. Sprinkle with paprika and pepper. Serve with fresh baked bread.

While the ling isn't the prettiest fish in the water, this freshwater cousin to the cod can—with the right preparation—grace your table and make believers of friends and family.

Pickled Northern

RECIPE FOR 1 QUART

2–3 lbs. northern fillets, cleaned with skin and rib bones removed

¼ cup salt

vinegar

Cut fillets across the grain into 1" strips. Loosely pack fish into a quart jar, pour in salt and enough vinegar to cover fish. Close jar and refrigerate for 5–6 days. Remove fish from refrigerator, drain and rinse with clean water.

BRINE

¾ cup sugar

¾ tablespoon pickling spice

1¼ cup vinegar

onion slices

Heat sugar, pickling spice and vinegar slowly until sugar is dissolved. Set aside to cool. Pack rinsed fish in clean jars alternating levels with large slices of onion. Pour in cooled brine to cover. Close jar and refrigerate. Fish can be eaten the next day.

Other fish may be substituted.

Baked Steelhead

1 fillet from a 6–10 lb. trout or salmon
lemon pepper
salt and pepper
½ cup real mayonnaise
½ cup sour cream
1 tablespoon lemon juice
¼ cup white wine
dill weed
½ teaspoon paprika

Preheat oven to 375°. Place fish in a single layer in a lightly greased 9x13 baking dish. Sprinkle with lemon pepper, salt and pepper. In a small bowl, whisk together mayonnaise, sour cream, lemon juice, wine and dill weed. Spread mixture over fish and sprinkle with paprika. Bake uncovered for 20 minutes or until fish flakes easily at its thickest part. Remove from oven, cover with foil and let rest for 5 minutes before serving.

Any large trout or salmon works just as well.

Broiled Lake Trout with Wine

1 fillet from a 2–3 lb. lake trout or other large trout, skin removed
½ cup white wine
1 tablespoon Dijon-style mustard
½ teaspoon seasoned salt
¼ teaspoon lemon pepper

Place fillets in a 9x13 glass baking dish. Pour wine over the fish and brush on the mustard. Sprinkle with seasonings. Place under broiler 12–15 minutes or until lightly browned and fish flakes easily at its thickest part.

NOTE

For outdoor or campfire grilling use heavy duty aluminum foil sealed tightly so it can be turned once.

An old fisherman told me "trout only live in beautiful places." Relive memories of those special reaches as you prepare your catch.

Grilled Brook Trout

4 brook trout cleaned, approximately 1 lb. each

MARINADE
¼ cup lemon juice
2 tablespoons vegetable oil
2 tablespoons sesame seeds
1 tablespoon tabasco sauce
½ teaspoon ground ginger
½ teaspoon salt

Combine all marinade ingredients and mix well. Place trout in a shallow baking dish and pour in the marinade. Cover and refrigerate 1 hour, turning several times. Remove fish from marinade, place on a well-greased rack and cook 4–5" over medium-hot coals for about 5 minutes. Turn, baste with marinade and cook an additional 5 minutes or until fish flakes easily at its thickest part.

I think "brookies" are the most beautiful fish I have ever chased. It's almost a shame to harvest them. It's kind of like killing a wood duck.

Broiled Walleye with Mustard Sauce

6 fillets, approximately ½ lb. each
4 tablespoons butter, divided
½ teaspoon salt
¼ teaspoon black pepper

SAUCE
2 tablespoons butter
1 tablespoon minced onion
1 tablespoon minced red bell pepper
1 tablespoon flour
1 cup milk
2 tablespoons hot & spicy mustard
¼ teaspoon seasoned salt

Grease a shallow 9x13 baking dish with 2 tablespoons butter. Place fillets in the dish, sprinkle with salt and pepper. Melt the remaining butter over the fish. Place under broiler approximately 4–6" from the heat source for 8–14 minutes.

Make the sauce while the fish is baking. Melt butter in a small saucepan. Add onion and red pepper and lightly sauté over medium heat. Stir in flour and slowly add milk, mustard and seasoned salt; continue stirring and cooking until sauce is thickened. Transfer fish to serving platter; pour sauce over fish and serve.

No excuses today, the fish cooperated and you feel great. Let's give thanks and eat.

Fried Walleye with Dill Sauce

4½ lbs. walleye fillets
2 tablespoons butter
2 tablespoons olive oil
½ cup flour
½ teaspoon salt
¼ teaspoon black pepper
¼ cup cornmeal

SAUCE
½ cup white wine
6 tablespoons sour cream
2 tablespoons chopped dill
1 tablespoon chopped fresh chives
1 tablespoon lemon zest
salt and pepper to taste

In a large skillet, combine butter and oil over medium heat. In a medium bowl, combine flour, salt, pepper and cornmeal. Dredge fillets. Fry fillets on first side until golden. Turn fillets and continue frying until done. Remove to a warm plate. Remove crumbs from skillet with paper towel and return it to medium heat. Add wine and cook for 6–8 minutes or until reduced by half. Stir in sour cream until smooth. Remove from heat and add herbs and lemon zest. Season with salt and pepper. Pour sauce over fish and serve.

Tip your beer and take a moment to toast an old mentor who took the time and made a difference in your life.

Grilled Walleye

6–8 walleye fillets with bones removed, skin and scales left on
4 tablespoons butter
2 cloves garlic, crushed
salt and pepper

In a small frying pan, melt butter and slowly sauté the garlic until lightly browned. Place fillets skin side down on greased rack 3" over coals. Sprinkle with salt and pepper. Baste with garlic butter and cover grill. Fish will be done when it flakes at its thickest part, about 8–10 minutes.

So many fish, so close to home. The mighty Missouri with its colorful history will whisper of days gone by.

Grilled Walleye with Vegetables

4 walleye fillets, approximately ½ lb. each
salt and pepper
1 teaspoon lemon pepper
4 tablespoons butter

VEGETABLE MIXTURE
1 medium zucchini, shredded
2 cups shredded carrots
2 cups chopped broccoli
½ cup diced onion
⅓ cup Parmesan cheese

For each fillet use a sheet of heavy-duty aluminum foil approximately 14x14". Combine all ingredients for vegetable mixture. Place a fillet in the center of each piece of foil, sprinkle with salt, pepper and lemon pepper. Top with 1 tablespoon butter. Place a quarter of the vegetable mixture over each fillet. Bring sides of the foil together over fish and fold, leaving ample room for steam circulation. Fold and crimp ends. Cook in covered grill over medium-hot coals for approximately 15 minutes.

For a quick camp meal that offers a whole meal in individual packets with no pots or pans. Cleanup is easy.

Poached Walleye

6½ lbs. walleye fillets
2 tablespoons butter
1 large onion, halved and thinly sliced
2 cloves garlic, minced
4 cups water
½ teaspoon dill weed
¾ cup skim milk
2 lemons, thinly sliced
¼ teaspoon black pepper

In a large skillet, melt butter over medium-high heat and sauté onion and garlic until lightly golden. Add water and dill weed and bring to a boil. Reduce heat and simmer uncovered for 4 minutes. Add milk, lemons and pepper. Place fillets in mixture and cover. Simmer for 12–15 minutes or until fish flakes easily at its thickest part. Remove fish and put on heated platter. Remove onions and lemon with slotted spoon and serve with fish.

A lean, no-fat preparation that doesn't lose flavor.

Stuffed Baked Walleye

1 6–8 lb. walleye, scaled, cleaned and gills removed
1 teaspoon salt
1 tablespoon lemon juice
8 slices fresh bread
1 medium onion, finely diced
2 stalks celery, finely diced
6 oz. fresh mushrooms, sliced
1 6-oz. can crab meat
⅛ teaspoon black pepper
¼ cup butter or margarine for basting

Preheat oven to 425°. Rub inside of fish with salt and sprinkle with lemon juice. Cut bread into ¼" cubes. Combine bread cubes with remaining ingredients except butter and mix well. Fill fish cavity with stuffing and fasten with skewers and string. Wrap in foil and bake in a shallow pan for 40 minutes. Open foil and bake 15 minutes longer, basting with butter during the last 15 minutes.

Try this elegant, mouth-watering recipe when your agenda calls for a special, festive treat.

Walleye & Wild Rice Stir Fry

2 lbs. walleye fillets, cut into bite-sized pieces
1 cup wild rice, uncooked
2 tablespoons butter
2 tablespoons vegetable oil
salt and pepper
seasoned salt
½ sweet red pepper, cut into julienne strips
½ green bell pepper, cut into julienne strips
½ cup baby carrots, cut into julienne strips
1 clove garlic, minced
1 small onion, chopped
2 tablespoons toasted sesame seeds
1 teaspoon teriyaki sauce

Prepare wild rice according to package directions. In a large nonstick skillet or wok, combine butter and oil and heat to 375°. Lightly season fish with salt, pepper and seasoned salt. Add fish and vegetables and stir fry gently for 4–6 minutes. Sprinkle with toasted sesame seeds. Add teriyaki sauce and serve individual portions over a bed of wild rice and enjoy.

There's plenty of flavor, color and variety in this dish, so simply serving it with warm, crusty bread will make a meal worth remembering.

Walleye Cheeks with Fettuccini

cheek meat from 10 2-lb. walleyes
1 8-oz. package of fettuccini
4 tablespoons butter
1 medium onion, minced
2 cloves garlic, minced
2 tablespoons flour
½ cup clam juice
2 cups light cream or half & half
½ teaspoon salt
¼ teaspoon white pepper
1 tablespoon chopped parsley
2 tablespoons grated Parmesan cheese

Begin by cooking pasta according to package directions.

At the same time, melt butter in a 2-qt. saucepan over medium-high heat. Add walleye cheeks and gently sauté 3–4 minutes. Remove from pan and set aside. Add onion and garlic and sauté 3–4 minutes. Reduce heat, stir in flour and lightly brown. Add clam juice; stir to blend. Add cream and stir until thickened. Add walleye cheeks, salt, pepper and parsley and cook an additional 3–4 minutes on low heat.

Serve over cooked fettuccini pasta; sprinkle with Parmesan cheese. Enjoy.

For the serious walleye connoisseur. Once you try this dish with those firm little morsels of walleye cheek meat, you'll find yourself keeping the cheeks from every cleaning.

Wild Rice & Fish Chowder

1½ lb. walleye, cut into bite-sized pieces
4 slices thick-cut bacon, chopped
1 bunch green onions, sliced
½ cup minced celery
2 medium potatoes, cubed
1 16-oz. can chicken broth
½ teaspoon dried dill weed
1½ teaspoon salt
½ teaspoon white pepper
4 tablespoons cornstarch
3 cups milk
1 cup cooked wild rice
1 cup cream
1 6-oz. can clams with juice
1 cup chopped spinach

Fry bacon in a large soup kettle until browned, then remove and drain. Add onions and celery and sauté until lightly browned. Add potatoes, broth, dill weed, salt and pepper, bring to boil, reduce heat and simmer on low for 10 minutes. Thicken by adding the cornstarch to the milk and blending until smooth. Stir into soup and again bring to boil. Reduce heat to low; then add wild rice, fish, bacon, cream, clams and spinach. Simmer an additional 6–8 minutes. Serve hot. Take the leftovers on your next ice fishing trip.

Ice fishing is better than no fishing. To liven up the day, take a kettle of this chowder to reheat on your camp stove and take the chill off.

Zucchini Baked Walleye

4–6 walleye fillets (all bones removed)
2 tablespoons butter
1 onion, minced
1 sweet red pepper, chopped
1 sweet yellow pepper, chopped
1 cup shredded carrots
3–4 potatoes, sliced
1 medium zucchini, shredded (about 2 cups)
½ teaspoon seasoned salt
¼ teaspoon black pepper

Arrange fillets in a buttered 9x13 glass baking dish. Melt butter in a frying pan and lightly sauté the onion, peppers and carrots. Layer the potatoes, zucchini and sautéed veggies on top of fish, sprinkle on salt and pepper.

SAUCE
2 tablespoons butter
2 tablespoons flour
1 cup milk
¼ teaspoon salt
2 tablespoons grated Parmesan cheese
1 cup shredded cojack or marble jack cheese
¼ teaspoon paprika

Melt the butter in the same frying pan used to sauté the veggies. Add flour, milk and salt; bring to a low boil while stirring. Pour over the prepared fish and veggies, sprinkle on the Parmesan cheese. Cover with foil and bake for 30 minutes at 350°. Remove foil and bake an additional 20 minutes. Sprinkle on the cojack cheese and paprika; return to the oven for 3 more minutes or until cheese is melted. Let rest for 3 minutes before serving.

Broiled Salmon Steaks

4 1"-thick salmon steaks
½ cup butter
2 large cloves garlic, minced
2 teaspoons lemon juice
1 teaspoon parsley flakes
½ teaspoon grated lemon peel

Place salmon on a greased broiler rack for approximately 8 minutes. In a small bowl combine the remaining ingredients and mix well. Brush salmon with mixture, turn and broil second side 8–10 minutes or until done. Baste with remaining mixture.

The best ventures into the outdoors never end. They live on in the memories we make, the feasts we prepare, the dreams we dream.

Cajun Salmon Pasta

4 4–6-oz. salmon fillets
2 tablespoons lemon juice
1 red pepper, minced
2 teaspoons minced jalapeno peppers
⅓ cup grated Parmesan cheese
1 tablespoon cornstarch
2 cloves garlic, minced
1 cup chicken broth
1 8-oz. package angel hair pasta

Arrange fillets in a shallow baking dish, sprinkle with lemon juice, cover tightly with foil and bake at 450° for 12–14 minutes or until fish flakes easily at its thickest part. Meanwhile, place peppers, cheese, cornstarch, garlic and chicken broth in blender and purée. Pour pepper mixture into a saucepan and cook over medium-high heat until it boils and then reduce heat. Stir in juices from baked salmon and simmer. Cook pasta according to directions on package. Spoon pasta onto plates and top with salmon. Spoon sauce over all.

This simple, yet elegant creation gives a spicy Cajun flavor to this unique pasta dish.

Grilled Salmon with Toasted Garlic

1 3–4-lb. salmon fillet with skin on and bones removed
4 tablespoons butter
4 cloves garlic, minced

In a small skillet, melt butter over medium heat. Add the minced garlic and sauté until garlic turns a light golden color. Remove from heat. Place salmon fillet on an oiled grill, skin side down. Baste with toasted garlic. Cover and cook for 12–15 minutes or until fish flakes easily at its thickest part. Serve with any remaining toasted garlic butter.

I have started serving this grilled salmon with the mango salsa recipe on page 89. For another salsa packed with flavor, substitute chopped cucumber for the mango.

Honey Grilled Salmon

SAUCE
¾ cup honey
¼ cup soy sauce
¼ cup brown sugar
¼ cup pineapple sauce
1 tablespoon lemon juice
2 tablespoons white vinegar
2 tablespoons olive oil
½ teaspoon cayenne pepper
½ teaspoon paprika
¼ teaspoon garlic powder

4 salmon fillets with skin and bone removed
2 tablespoons olive oil
salt and pepper

Combine all sauce ingredients in a saucepan and cook over low heat. Rub salmon with olive oil, lightly season with salt and pepper. Grill over medium-high heat, basting lightly with the sauce. Salmon is done when it flakes easily at its thickest part. Smother with remaining sauce and enjoy.

Friends and family will fall hook, line and sinker when you present them with this tasty creation.

Poached Salmon & Mango Salsa

POACHED SALMON

**4 salmon fillets with all bones removed, cut into 4"
segments**
salt
lemon pepper seasoning
4 sprigs fresh cut dill
2 cups chicken broth

Lightly butter the bottom of a 9x13 glass baking dish. Place salmon fillets
in dish, sprinkle with salt and lemon pepper and fresh cut dill. Pour chicken
broth in pan until just shy of covering fillets. Bake at 350° for 20 minutes
or until fish flakes at its thickest part. Remove from oven, let rest for 2–3
minutes. Remove from pan, skin will easily slide off. Serve hot with the
chilled mango salsa on the side.

MANGO SALSA

1 ripe mango, peeled, seeded and diced
¼ cup finely chopped red bell pepper
¼ cup finely chopped red onion
1½ teaspoons minced garlic
½ cup rice wine vinegar
2 tablespoons finely chopped fresh cilantro
⅛ teaspoon salt

You can make this well in advance of your dinner. Combine the mango,
red bell pepper, onion and garlic in a bowl and stir to combine. Add the
vinegar, cilantro and salt and stir well. Cover and refrigerate for 2–4 hours
before serving.

This will satisfy your taste for adventure.

Salmon Croquettes

1 pint canned salmon
1 cup crushed cornflakes
½ cup milk
2 eggs
3 tablespoons butter
4 green onions, thinly sliced
½ teaspoon seasoned salt
⅛ teaspoon black pepper

SAUCE
2 tablespoons butter
2 tablespoons flour
1½ cups milk
½ cup shredded cheddar cheese
1 clove garlic, minced
1 tablespoon minced green chilies
dash of ground pepper

In a medium bowl combine cornflakes, milk, eggs, butter, onions, salmon, salt and pepper. Place mixture into a large, greased 6-count muffin tin. Bake uncovered at 350° for 15 minutes.

To make the sauce, melt butter in a medium saucepan, then stir in flour until smooth. Stir in milk and bring to a boil. Reduce heat, stir and cook for an additional minute or until thickened. Add cheese, garlic, chilies and pepper. Cook and stir until cheese is melted. Serve over salmon croquettes.

Never worry about leftovers when you share this recipe. The salmon and sauce blend a taste loved by everyone.

Salmon Linguini

1 lb. salmon fillets, skin and bone removed
3 cups chicken broth
3 teaspoons olive oil
1 bunch (8–10) green onions, thinly sliced (use white and light green stems only)
1 sweet red bell pepper, chopped
1 cup frozen peas
1 teaspoon salt
¼ teaspoon white pepper
1 16-oz. box linguini
Parmesan cheese, grated

In a large pan arrange fillets in a single layer, pour broth over top and heat to simmer over medium heat. Cover and poach 6–8 minutes. Do not overcook; salmon is done when it flakes easily at its thickest part. Remove carefully from the pan and place on a plate. Cut into bite-sized pieces. Save ½ cup broth. In the same pan heat olive oil, sauté onions and red pepper until they begin to soften, about 5 minutes. Add peas and cook for an additional minute. Reduce heat, add salmon, salt and pepper and reserved ½ cup broth.

Cook linguini according to directions on package, then drain and combine with salmon mixture. Reheat if necessary, serve immediately with grated fresh Parmesan cheese.

When you grill or poach salmon, always cook extra to be used in salads for future meals.

Salmon Loaf

1 pint canned salmon
2 slices bread, crumbed
¾ cup milk
2 eggs, beaten
1 medium onion, minced
1 stalk celery, chopped
½ green pepper, chopped
1 teaspoon lemon juice
2 tablespoons melted butter
½ teaspoon parsley flakes
1 teaspoon Dijon-style mustard
¼ teaspoon black pepper

Drain salmon and place in medium bowl. Add all remaining ingredients and mix well. Pour into well-greased loaf pan. Bake at 350° for 1 hour.

The veggies and mustard pack a unique texture and flavor into this traditional loaf.

Salmon Pâté

1 15-oz. can salmon, drained
1 8-oz. package light cream cheese
½ teaspoon liquid smoke
3 tablespoons grated onion
½ teaspoon prepared horseradish
½ teaspoon cayenne pepper

In a medium bowl, cream the cheese until smooth. Add remaining ingredients and mix well. Cover and chill for at least 1 hour. Serve with toasted bagels and/or crackers.

Simple and versatile. A treat for any occasion.

Salmon Pepper Pasta

4 4-oz. salmon fillets
¼ teaspoon lemon pepper
2 tablespoons lemon juice
2 tablespoons butter
2 cloves garlic, minced
1 red bell pepper, chopped
6 green onions, sliced
1½ cups chicken broth
¼ cup grated Parmesan cheese
1 tablespoon cornstarch
1 16-oz. box angel hair pasta

Preheat oven to 450°. Place fish in a shallow baking dish. Sprinkle with lemon pepper and lemon juice. Cover with foil and bake for 12–16 minutes, or until fish flakes at its thickest part.

Meanwhile, in a medium saucepan, melt butter and sauté the garlic, red pepper and green onions over medium heat until tender. Add chicken broth and Parmesan cheese. Stir in cornstarch. Reduce heat and simmer until ready to serve.

Cook pasta according to directions on package. Mix half the sauce with drained pasta. Flake fish in individual servings and drizzle with remaining sauce.

You will create a new tradition when you set this dinner before your guests. You'll get requests for this meal again and again.

Salmon Puffs

SALMON STUFFING
16 oz. drained canned salmon with skin removed
2 cups minced celery
¼ cup mayonnaise
2 tablespoons minced green onion
2 tablespoons sweet pickle relish

Combine all stuffing ingredients in a medium bowl and refrigerate.

PUFF SHELLS
1 cup boiling water
½ cup butter
¼ teaspoon salt
1 cup flour
4 eggs

Preheat oven to 450°. Combine water, butter and salt in a saucepan and bring to a boil. Add flour and stir vigorously until mixture forms a ball in the pan. Remove from heat, add eggs one at a time and beat until dough is stiff. Drop by level teaspoonful on a cookie sheet and bake for 10 minutes. Reduce heat to 350° and continue baking for an additional 10 minutes. Remove from the oven and allow to cool. Cut tops off each puff and fill with 1 teaspoon of salmon stuffing. Replace top of puff and enjoy.

Served as an appetizer, this recipe is relatively simple and well worth the effort.

Salmon Scramble

2 cups smoked salmon
8 large fresh eggs
3 tablespoons milk
4 tablespoons chopped fresh chives
4 tablespoons butter
1 large onion, chopped
4 tablespoons chopped red pepper

In a large bowl beat eggs, add milk and chives. Melt butter in a large frying pan over medium heat. Add onion and red pepper and sauté until golden. Add beaten egg mixture, blend and cook lightly. Add salmon and cook until eggs are cooked through, yet moist. Season with salt and pepper. Serve with toasted bagels or English muffins.

One bite of this heavenly treat will conjure up instant memories of cool mornings, bent rods and wild runs of sleek, silver salmon.

Smoked Salmon Spread

1 lb. smoked salmon
1 cup Hellman's Mayonnaise
2 tablespoons sweet pickle relish
2 tablespoons chopped parsley
1 tablespoon hot & spicy mustard
4 green onions, chopped
1 stalk celery, minced
1 clove garlic, minced
Dash of Worcestershire sauce

Remove all skin and bones from the salmon. Shred or flake the fish, add all remaining ingredients and blend well. Cover and chill, preferably overnight. Serve on a toasted onion bagel, crackers or garlic toast.

Used as a spread on a toasted bagel or appetizer on crackers, this salmon is packed with flavor. As the ingredients blend, it's always better the second day.

Baked Halibut

4 lbs. filleted halibut or other large, white-fleshed fish
2 tablespoons butter
2 large onions, sliced
2 cloves garlic, minced
1 sweet red pepper, chopped
1 stalk celery, chopped
½ teaspoon each, salt and black pepper
2 cups mayonnaise
1 cup sour cream
2 cups grated fresh Parmesan cheese
1 cup provolone cheese, grated
2 tablespoons lemon juice

Melt butter in a skillet over medium-high heat. Sauté onions, garlic, red pepper and celery until soft and partially caramelized. Remove from heat and place about half of the veggies in a large 9x13 glass baking pan. Place fillets in a single layer over veggies, sprinkle with salt and black pepper, top with remaining veggies.

In a large bowl, combine mayo, sour cream, cheeses and lemon juice. Spread mixture over fish, cover with foil and bake at 350° for 30 minutes. Remove foil and bake an additional 5–7 minutes. Remove from oven, let rest for 3–4 minutes before serving. Serve with fresh hot rolls or bread.

I'm still working on bringing in that really big halibut. Each summer I give it another try. I just hope I'm not too old and frail when he finally shows up.

Grilled Halibut

4¾ lbs. halibut steaks
¼ cup olive oil
1 oz. Jack Daniels bourbon
½ teaspoon soy sauce
salt and pepper

Combine olive oil, bourbon, soy sauce and halibut steaks in a gallon-sized sealable bag. Seal and refrigerate for 2–4 hours, turning occasionally. Prepare grill and put a light coat of oil on grill plate. Remove fish from marinade and place on grill over hot coals. Grill 6–8 minutes per side, basting occasionally with remaining marinade. Salt and pepper to taste. Serve with oven-roasted potatoes.

I use this basic marinade for fish, fowl and venison. The oil seals in the juices and flavor while the soy and whiskey give it that added smoky finish.

Poached Halibut Appetizers

**2 lbs. halibut or other white-fleshed fish, cut into
bite-sized pieces**

MARINADE
3 tablespoons honey
2 tablespoons lemon juice
1 clove garlic, minced
3 tablespoons minced parsley
¼ teaspoon salt
⅛ teaspoon tabasco sauce
2 tablespoons olive oil

POACHING INGREDIENTS
6 cups water
½ cup dry white wine
1 medium onion, sliced
2 lemon slices
½ teaspoon salt

In a small bowl combine all marinade ingredients and stir until blended.

In large pot or kettle combine poaching ingredients and bring to a
boil over medium-high heat. Add fish, cover and simmer 6–8 minutes.
Remove from heat, let stand 5 minutes, remove fish from pot with slotted
spoons. Place in a serving dish and drizzle with the marinade. Refrigerate
until served.

*You can never have enough of these tender morsels. They always seem to
vanish, no matter the number of people.*

Crab Cakes

2 lbs. crab meat
½ lb. fresh white-fleshed fish
½ cup cream
1 tablespoon hot & spicy mustard
1 tablespoon sesame oil
2 tablespoons minced parsley
2 tablespoons minced green onion
1 tablespoon minced basil
½ teaspoon salt
¼ teaspoon black pepper
1 tablespoon lemon juice
4 tablespoons olive oil

Check crab meat and remove shell bits. Grind fish in a food processor, then add cream and purée. Place mixture in a large bowl; add other ingredients except olive oil. Form the mixture into patties; sauté in a large frying pan with hot olive oil until golden brown. Finish by baking in a 450° oven for 4–5 minutes.

I came upon this treat in my attempt to discover something new every day. I recently started adding wild rice as a nutritious filler.

Ketchikan Crab Mornay

SAUCE
2 cups whipping cream
2 cups half & half
½ cup butter
¼ cup flour
¼ cup dry white wine
½ cup grated Parmesan cheese
salt
white pepper

Combine whipping cream and half & half in a large saucepan. Bring to a boil, taking care not to scorch. Heat butter in a small skillet. Stir in flour until smooth and golden. Stir in 4 tablespoons of hot cream, then add back into cream mixture in saucepan and bring to boil, stirring constantly. Add wine and cheese and simmer over low heat until blended. Season with salt and pepper.

2 lbs. crab meat
4 tablespoons dry bread crumbs
3 tablespoons melted butter
paprika

Spread ¼ cup sauce in the bottom of each of 8 individual casseroles. Sprinkle 4 oz. of crab meat in each casserole, cover with ¼ cup sauce, sprinkle with bread crumbs, drizzle with butter, sprinkle with paprika. Bake at 375° for 10–12 minutes.

Some days in life far exceed our expectations; this is one of those extraordinary experiences.

Seafood Gallimaufry (Fish Stew)

1 lb. halibut or similar firm, white-fleshed fish (cut into bite-sized pieces)

2 cups shrimp

1 cup clams

2 tablespoons vegetable oil

half of a green pepper, chopped

1 medium onion, chopped

1 clove garlic, crushed

1 large can tomatoes

1 large can tomato sauce

1 medium zucchini, sliced

½ cup white wine

3 tablespoons parsley

½ teaspoon salt

¼ teaspoon thyme

In a soup pot, heat oil over medium heat. Sauté green pepper, onion and garlic until tender. Add tomatoes, tomato sauce, zucchini, wine, parsley, salt and thyme. Bring to a boil. Reduce heat and simmer for 20 minutes. Add halibut, shrimp and clams, and cook for an additional 10 minutes. Serve with steamed white rice.

Served with a premium beer, this "stoup" (stew/soup) will warm you on a cold, blustery winter evening.

Seafood Newberg

1 lb. cod, sole, snapper or bass
1 lb. lobster, crab meat or scallops
4 tablespoons butter
3 tablespoons lemon juice
1 tablespoon flour
1 teaspoon salt
½ teaspoon paprika
⅛ teaspoon cayenne pepper
3 cups cream, divided
3 egg yolks
2 tablespoons sherry

Melt butter in heavy frying pan over medium heat. Cut seafood into 1" pieces and lightly sauté for about 5 minutes. Add lemon juice. Mix flour, salt, paprika and cayenne pepper; add to seafood. Slowly add 2 cups of cream. Stir and bring mixture to a simmer. Combine egg yolks with the remaining cup of cream, blend with seafood, stir until slightly thickened. Add sherry just before serving. Serve over rice.

We're not here for a long time, but we can sure make it a good time. Kick back and indulge.

Shrimp Casserole

½ lb. small shrimp, peeled and deveined
3 lbs. yellow squash, chopped
1 onion, chopped
4 tablespoons butter
1 cup heavy whipping cream
8 oz. cojack or cheddar cheese, cubed
1 tablespoon cornstarch
½ teaspoon salt
¼ teaspoon black pepper
10 Keebler crackers, crushed

Preheat oven to 350°. In a large pot of salted water, boil squash and onion until tender. In a saucepan combine butter and cream, stir constantly over low heat. Mix in cheese, cornstarch, salt and pepper. Stir until sauce thickens. Place squash and onions in a 2-quart baking dish. Mix in shrimp and cheese sauce. Sprinkle with cracker crumbs. Bake uncovered for 20–30 minutes.

Last year we caught our own shrimp in the inland waterway off the coast of Alaska. The crew I cooked them for thought this feast was the highlight of the trip.

Venison, Elk &
Other Big Game

A Few Helpful Hints about Big Game

North America's white-tailed deer population has practically exploded over the past several decades. Getting a license or bagging a deer isn't nearly as difficult as it may have been 30 years ago and just about anyone who has the desire can get fresh venison. The following pages contain a variety of recipes and methods for cooking your trophy.

Tips for good venison: Great-tasting venison begins in the field and is the result of a well-planned hunt and proper preparation. In other words, be prepared for the task at hand before taking the shot.

- A downed animal must be field-dressed immediately and allowed to cool.

- If the temperature is above 40° the animal should be skinned and cooled.

- The carcass can be hung and aged for up to a week at temperatures near freezing. Trim all visible fat, tissue, membrane and silver skin from the meat during processing.

- All venison does not taste the same. Meat from different species of game varies by age, diet, field processing and preparation.

- Venison is easy to overcook, so cut all steaks at least 1" thick.

- Venison is a dense meat; a little goes a long way.

- Preheat skillet, frying pan, grill or oven before cooking venison.

- Brush or coat meat with olive or vegetable oil prior to frying or grilling for quick browning and to retain natural juices.

- Cook venison quickly at high heat to keep it from drying out.

- Venison should be served rare to medium-rare. As venison cooks past medium-rare it toughens up and loses flavor.

- If you plan to share your bounty, do it early; don't wait until it has been in the freezer for months.

The recipes that follow can be used with any animals considered big game. The rich red texture of venison is versatile and you may substitute elk, moose, white-tailed deer, mule deer, caribou or pronghorn at will; just tend your fire and serve it rare.

Apple Roast Venison

1 boneless loin roast (approximately 3 lbs.)
2 tablespoons canola or vegetable oil
1 cup water, plus 2 tablespoons
½ teaspoon Worcestershire sauce
1 beef bouillon cube
1 clove garlic, crushed
1 teaspoon seasoned salt
1 large tart apple, quartered
1 large onion, sliced
2 tablespoons flour
¼ teaspoon black pepper

In a large skillet or frying pan heat oil over medium-high heat and brown roast on all sides. Transfer meat to a suitable crock pot or slow cooker. Add 1 cup water, Worcestershire sauce, bouillon and garlic. Sprinkle seasoned salt over meat and place the apple pieces and onion on top. Cover and cook on low for 6–8 hours. Remove meat and onion to a platter, cover with foil. Strain cooking juices into a saucepan and discard the apple. Bring liquid to a boil. Meanwhile, combine the flour, pepper and remaining 2 tablespoons water and stir or shake until smooth. Stir into cooking liquid and reduce heat as gravy thickens. Slice meat; top with onions and gravy.

Still-hunting in a mountain forest can reveal the mysteries of life.

Bourbon Venison Steaks

4 loin steaks, cut 1" thick
2 tablespoons oil
1 cup sliced mushrooms
1 large onion, chopped
1 cup water
2 beef bouillon cubes
¼ cup bourbon
½ cup sour cream
salt and pepper to taste

In a large skillet, brown steaks in oil over medium-high heat for approximately 5 minutes per side. When the steaks are turned, add mushrooms and onion. Reduce heat and add water, bouillon, bourbon and salt and pepper to taste. Simmer for 15–20 minutes. Put meat on a platter. Stir in sour cream and return meat to the skillet to simmer for 5 minutes. Serve over rice, potatoes or noodles.

Lord, just once let me shoot a buck so big that when I tell about it, I don't have to lie.

Brandied Venison Steak

4 steaks cut from loin, 1" thick
3 tablespoons butter
1 oz. brandy
1 tablespoon Worcestershire sauce
¼ teaspoon salt
¼ teaspoon freshly ground black pepper

Melt butter in a large frying pan over medium-high heat. Place meat in pan, sear quickly on both sides. Reduce heat to medium and cook for an additional 2–3 minutes per side. Add brandy, Worcestershire sauce, salt and pepper and stir to blend. Simmer for an additional 2 minutes. Serve immediately with rice, potatoes or squash.

To me and many like-minded souls, hunting is a passion. I'm sure there are more important pursuits in life, but I'll be darned if I can think of what they might be.

Country Fried Venison

2 lbs. round steak from deer, elk, antelope
1 teaspoon salt
½ teaspoon freshly ground black pepper
2 eggs, beaten with 1 tablespoon water
1 cup finely crushed saltine cracker crumbs
⅓ cup vegetable oil
1 cup sliced fresh mushrooms
1 large onion, sliced
1 sweet red pepper, chopped
2 cups chicken stock or bouillon

Pound steak well before cutting into serving pieces. Sprinkle salt and pepper on each side of meat. Dip in egg mixture, roll in cracker crumbs and lightly fry in vegetable oil in heavy frying pan over moderate heat.

Remove meat from frying pan and layer in roasting pan or Dutch oven. Add mushrooms, onion, red pepper and heated chicken broth. Cover and bake at 350° for 1 hour or until tender. Uncover and continue to bake until juices are absorbed.

Feast on this tasty tradition and enjoy the flashback of wide racks with long drop tines.

Dutch Oven Goulash

1½ lbs. cubed venison
2 tablespoons vegetable oil
1 large onion, chopped
1 can beer
1 cup water
2 beef bouillon cubes
1 tablespoon tomato paste
1 teaspoon paprika
½ teaspoon salt
¼ teaspoon black pepper
3 medium potatoes
1 can sauerkraut

Heat oil in Dutch oven over hot coals. Add meat to brown. When meat is turned, add onion. Add beer, water, bouillon, tomato paste and seasonings. Cover and simmer for 1 hour. Cut potatoes into 1" pieces and add to Dutch oven along with sauerkraut and juice. Cook, covered, an additional 30 minutes. Uncover and allow to cook for an additional 10–15 minutes, or until goulash is thickened.

Served in deer camp among the stars, with coyotes yapping from the next butte, this dish helps sleep come easy.

Grilled Venison Backstrap
with Crab Sauce & Wild Rice

1 fillet of backstrap or saddle, cut in half
¼ cup olive oil
1 oz. bourbon
1 teaspoon steak seasoning

CRAB SAUCE
½ cup butter
1 teaspoon minced onion
1 6-oz. can fancy crab meat
1 cup cream
¼ cup white zinfandel
3 egg yolks, beaten
salt and pepper

1 cup wild rice, cooked to directions on package

To prepare the meat, place oil and bourbon in a gallon-sized sealable bag. Sprinkle the steak seasoning on the meat, place meat in bag, seal and turn to coat. Place the meat in the refrigerator 4–6 hours. Start preparing the wild rice 1 hour before serving time. Remove meat from bag. Grill over hot coals 4–6 minutes per side. Serve medium-rare; do not overcook.

Prepare the crab sauce by melting butter in a medium saucepan over medium heat. Add onion and sauté gently for 2–3 minutes. Add crab meat and continue cooking. In a separate bowl combine the cream, wine and egg yolks. Add to the saucepan, stirring constantly until the sauce thickens. Add salt and pepper to taste.

Plan meal so all items are finished simultaneously, serve hot.

The camp cook has just offered his best.

Grilled Venison Mushroom Steak

4 1"-thick steaks, cut from loin
5 tablespoons butter, divided
2 teaspoons flour
½ lb. fresh mushrooms, sliced
1 teaspoon Worcestershire sauce
½ cup sherry
½ teaspoon black pepper, divided
½ teaspoon salt

Melt 4 tablespoons of butter in a large frying pan over medium heat. Add flour and blend with butter. Add the mushrooms and sauté for 4–5 minutes. Stir in the Worcestershire sauce, sherry and ¼ teaspoon of pepper. Reduce heat and simmer until thickened.

Rub both sides of each steak with remaining butter and season with salt and remaining pepper. Place meat on hot grill for 3–4 minutes per side. Remove steaks from grill. Top with mushroom sauce and serve.

Eat, sleep, hunt. Repeat.

Honey Glazed Venison Roast

1 boneless venison leg roast, approximately 3–4 lbs.
1 onion, chopped
2 teaspoons fresh parsley
2 teaspoons fresh thyme
1 teaspoon sage
1 teaspoon grated lemon peel
1 large clove of garlic, minced
½ teaspoon salt
½ cup honey
2 tablespoons lemon juice
salt and pepper

In a medium bowl combine onion, herbs, lemon peel, garlic and salt. Blend honey and lemon juice in a separate bowl. Sprinkle meat with salt and pepper, rub with onion herb mixture, then brush with honey and lemon.

Roast on a rack in an oiled pan at 350°, allowing 20–25 minutes per pound. Baste with honey lemon mixture every 20–30 minutes. Meat is done when internal temperature reaches 145°. Let roast stand for 5–10 minutes before carving.

Every day without a tombstone is a milestone.

Roast Venison Hoagies

1 3–4-lb. venison roast
1½ teaspoons dried basil
1½ teaspoons dried oregano
1¼ teaspoons salt
¼ teaspoon black pepper
1 12-oz. jar pickled peppers, drained with juice
    reserved, stems and seeds removed
2 cloves garlic, minced
1 large onion, chopped
1 green pepper, chopped
¼ cup water
2 beef bouillon cubes
6–8 hoagie buns
½ cup shredded cheddar cheese

Cut roast into large chunks. Combine basil, oregano, salt, pepper, pickled peppers, garlic, onion and green pepper in a large bowl. Add water and bouillon to crock pot. Layer the meat, sprinkling some of the onion and pepper mixture over each layer of meat. Top with remaining mixture and juice from pickled peppers. Cover and cook on low 8–9 hours or until meat is tender. Shred meat. Serve in buns. Sprinkle with cheddar cheese.

One of the best meals on a bun you will ever eat.

Simple Venison Roast

1 4–5-lb. roast, cut from loin
1 teaspoon black pepper
1 tablespoon Cajun-Creole seasoning
½ teaspoon garlic powder
1 teaspoon dry mustard
½ cup water

In a small bowl combine all seasonings and blend thoroughly. Rub mixture over the meat, place in a slow cooker or crock pot and add water. Cook on low for 8–10 hours or until meat is tender. Remove from pot, strain the juices and serve with meat. Serve with your favorite pasta, vegetable and bread.

When the season has been good and your freezer is full, share your harvest with your older friends who don't get out much anymore.

Skillet Venison Sausage & Peppers

1 lb. country-style venison sausage, cut into ½" pieces
4 tablespoons oil
1 sweet red bell pepper, chopped
1 green bell pepper, chopped
1 yellow or orange bell pepper, chopped
1 large onion, chopped
1 cup water
1 package golden onion soup mix
4 cups cooked wild rice

Brown sausage chunks in a large skillet in oil over medium-high heat. Add peppers and onion when sausage is turned. Cook until onion is translucent. Combine the water and soup mix in a small bowl, add to skillet, reduce heat. Cover and simmer for 5 minutes. Serve over the bed of cooked wild rice.

This dinner is popular in deer camp and also in the ice house in winter. Its simple, hearty aroma will attract hunters and fishermen alike.

Venison Burgundy & Noodles

1½ lbs. venison loin cut into ¼" strips
1 tablespoon olive oil
1 teaspoon butter
1 small onion, diced
2 cups fresh mushrooms, quartered
1 beef bouillon cube
¾ cup red wine
1 cup water
1 bay leaf
1 whole clove
¼ teaspoon salt
⅛ teaspoon black pepper
2 tablespoons flour
¼ cup water
1 package wide noodles, prepared according to directions on package

In Dutch oven or nonstick skillet, brown meat in olive oil and butter over medium-high heat. Add onion when meat is turned. Add mushrooms, bouillon, wine, water, bay leaf, clove, salt and pepper. Bring to a boil, then reduce heat. Cover and simmer for 1 hour or until meat is tender. Blend flour and water and stir into meat mixture. Stir for an additional 2–3 minutes to thicken. Remove and discard clove and bay leaf. Serve over prepared noodles.

Tantalize your senses with this bubbling creation.

Venison Chili

2 lbs. venison loin, cubed
4 tablespoons cooking oil
1 large onion, chopped
1 green pepper, chopped
1 red pepper, chopped
3 stalks of celery, chopped
1 32-oz. can peeled whole tomatoes
1 46-oz. can V-8 juice
1 32-oz. can chili beans
1 16-oz. can red kidney beans
1 3-oz. can jalapeno peppers, sliced
1 12-oz. can tomato paste
1 teaspoon salt
½ teaspoon black pepper
1 teaspoon hot chili pepper
minced raw onions
grated cheddar cheese

Brown meat in oil in a heavy frying pan over medium-high heat. Add onion and cook until lightly brown. Transfer meat and onion to soup kettle. Add remaining ingredients and simmer, covered, for 2–3 hours, stirring occasionally. Serve with freshly minced raw onions and grated cheddar cheese sprinkled on top.

Hot chili and good friends sharing a sip of rye somewhere along the Lewis and Clark trail. Life is good.

Venison Meat Loaf

1½ lbs. ground venison
1 egg
½ cup sour cream
2 tablespoons Worcestershire sauce
2 tablespoons onion soup mix
¼ cup grated Parmesan cheese
2 cups Italian style bread crumbs
½ teaspoon salt
¼ teaspoon black pepper

Preheat oven to 375°. In a large bowl, combine all the ingredients and knead to blend well. Form mixture and place in a 9x5 loaf or bread pan. Cover with foil. Bake for 1 hour. Remove foil and bake for an additional 10 minutes. Remove from oven and let rest for 10 minutes before slicing and serving.

This meat loaf has never been entered in a contest but everyone who eats it gives it a blue ribbon.

Venison Mulligan

2 lbs. venison, cut into 1" cubes
⅓ cup flour
¼ teaspoon pepper
½ teaspoon seasoned salt
4 tablespoons cooking oil
½ cup minced onion
4 cups water
2 beef bouillon cubes
1 cup frozen peas
4 medium potatoes, quartered
4 carrots, sliced
2 tablespoons chopped parsley

Mix flour, pepper and salt; dredge venison cubes. Heat cooking oil in a heavy frying pan over medium heat and brown meat. When pieces are turned add onion. When venison is browned add water and bouillon; cover and simmer for 30 minutes. Add peas, potatoes, carrots and parsley. Cook 30 more minutes or until everything is tender. The mixture can be thickened to the desired consistency with the remaining flour mixture. Salt to taste.

MULLIGAN WITH DUMPLINGS
2 cups flour
1 tablespoon baking powder
½ teaspoon salt
½ teaspoon seasoned salt
1 tablespoon butter
¾ cup milk

To add dumplings to your already sumptuous meal, sift together flour, baking powder and salts; cut in butter. Fold in milk. Drop tablespoonfuls of batter on top of the slowly bubbling mulligan. Cover and steam for 15–20 minutes.

Venison Oscar

4 1"-thick venison fillets, cut from the tenderloin
8 asparagus spears
3 tablespoons butter, divided
4 oz. white wine
1 tablespoon finely minced onion
1 tablespoon finely minced green pepper
1 4-oz. can tomato sauce
¼ teaspoon salt
⅛ teaspoon black pepper
8 medallions preboiled lobster or king crab meat

Heat asparagus in lightly salted water. Melt 2 tablespoons of the butter over medium heat and sauté fillets in heavy frying pan for 4–5 minutes on each side. Remove meat from pan and keep warm. Deglaze pan with white wine, add onion and green pepper and toss over medium heat for several minutes. Add remaining 1 tablespoon butter, then stir in tomato sauce, salt and pepper. Add lobster or crab and simmer until hot. Serve meat on heated platter, top with asparagus and seafood medallions. Pour remaining sauce over all.

Serve with baked potato.

For a special dinner when elegance is required.

Venison Pepper Steak

2 lbs. venison round steak
½ cup flour
½ teaspoon seasoned salt
½ teaspoon black pepper
4 tablespoons vegetable oil
1 large onion, sliced
½ lb. fresh mushrooms, sliced
1 tablespoon Worcestershire sauce
1 tablespoon prepared mustard
1 large green bell pepper, sliced
1 large red bell pepper, sliced
1 cup water

Cut meat into 1"-wide strips that are 3–4" long. Mix flour, salt and pepper. Dredge meat to coat. Heat oil over medium-high heat in large frying pan and lightly brown meat. Add onion, mushrooms, Worcestershire sauce, mustard and bell pepper. Stir and continue cooking for 10 minutes. Add water, cover and simmer 30 minutes or until meat is tender.

This tasty tradition will bring back memories of hunts past, with stories of old bucks told until sleep comes.

Venison Sauerbraten

1 4 lb. round venison loin roast
2 teaspoons salt
1 teaspoon ground ginger
2½ cups water
2 cups cider vinegar
2 onions, sliced
¼ cup sugar
2 tablespoons mixed pickling spices
1 teaspoon whole peppercorns
8 whole cloves
2 bay leaves
2 tablespoons vegetable oil
14 gingersnap cookies, crushed

Combine the salt and ginger and rub over roast. Place meat in deep container with cover. In a medium saucepan, combine water, vinegar, onions, sugar, spices, peppercorns, cloves and bay leaves and bring to a boil. Cool marinade and pour over meat. Cover and refrigerate for 2 days, turning twice a day. Remove meat and reserve marinade.

Heat oil in a Dutch oven over medium-high heat. Brown roast on all sides. Pour 1 cup of marinade over roast. Heat oven to 325°. Place roast in oven for 3 hours. Transfer meat to a heated platter.

Strain cooking juices and add reserved marinade until mixture equals 3 cups. Over high heat bring to a rolling boil. Add gingersnap cookies and reduce heat to simmer until gravy thickens. Slice meat and serve with gravy and potato dumplings.

The unique flavor of supper will be savored long after the dishes are cleared away.

Venison Sloppy Joe

2½ lbs. ground venison, elk or moose burger
2 tablespoons vegetable oil
5 stalks celery, chopped
1 large onion, chopped
1 can tomato soup
1 can chicken gumbo soup
2 tablespoons hot & spicy mustard
1 teaspoon chili powder
2 tablespoons brown sugar
2 teaspoons salt
¼ teaspoon pepper
12 large hamburger buns

Brown the meat in vegetable oil in a deep kettle or Dutch oven over medium-high heat. Add celery and onion and cook an additional 3–4 minutes. Add remaining ingredients, stir to blend and simmer over medium-low heat for 1½ hours. Serve on toasted hamburger buns.

This old faithful can be made ahead of time and frozen for a quick, tasty meal anytime.

Venison Stew

3 lbs. boneless venison round roast, cut into 1" cubes
2 medium potatoes, quartered
2 medium onions, chopped
2 cloves garlic, minced
3 stalks celery, chopped
½ lb. baby carrots
1 12-oz. can V-8 Juice
½ cup cooking sherry
1 tablespoon brown sugar
⅓ cup quick-cooking tapioca
1 teaspoon salt
½ teaspoon dried basil
¼ teaspoon black pepper
1 can cut green beans

In a Dutch oven, combine the meat, potatoes, onions, garlic, celery and carrots. In a medium bowl combine V-8 Juice, sherry, brown sugar, tapioca, salt, basil and pepper; pour over mixture in Dutch oven and bake at 325° for 2 hours or until meat is tender. Add beans and cook an additional 20 minutes. Serve with fresh warm bread.

Stews offer something for everyone. You may want to develop your own variation but this recipe will help you get started. As for me, I never make it the same way twice.

Venison Stir Fry

1 lb. venison round steak
2 tablespoons cornstarch
2 teaspoons sugar
6 tablespoons soy sauce
¼ cup white wine
2 tablespoons vegetable oil, divided
3 cups broccoli florets
2 medium carrots, sliced
½ cup chopped red pepper
½ cup chopped onion
2 cups pea pods
1 8-oz. can sliced water chestnuts (undrained)

In a medium bowl combine cornstarch, sugar, soy sauce and wine. Cut meat into thin strips, add to mixture, toss to coat and set aside.

In a large skillet over medium heat, add 1 tablespoon oil and stir fry vegetables for 1 minute. Stir in water chestnuts, cover and simmer for 5 minutes. Remove from pan and keep warm. In same skillet, stir fry meat in remaining oil for approximately 4 minutes or until done. Return vegetables to skillet, toss and serve over hot steaming rice.

Stir fry offers a wholesome, attractive meal not generally steeped in the tradition of basic venison.

Venison Stroganoff

2 lbs. venison, cut into 1" cubes
½ cup pancake mix
¼ teaspoon black pepper
⅛ teaspoon seasoned salt
4 tablespoons cooking oil
2 cloves garlic, minced
1 large onion, chopped
half of a red bell pepper, chopped
2 cups water
2 beef bouillon cubes
1 teaspoon salt
8 oz. fresh mushrooms, sliced
1 cup sour cream

In a medium bowl, mix pancake mix, pepper and seasoned salt and dredge meat. Heat cooking oil in a heavy frying pan or Dutch oven and brown the meat. When meat pieces are turned, add garlic, onion and red pepper. When meat is browned add water, bouillon, salt and mushrooms, cover and simmer for 45 minutes. Add sour cream and simmer briefly. Serve over hot buttered noodles.

A favorite in every deer hunter's cookbook. The rich flavor of stroganoff is tough to beat.

Venison Summer Sausage

TO MAKE 100 LBS. OF SAUSAGE

40 lbs. venison, all fat, membrane and silver skin removed

30 lbs. beef chuck

30 lbs. pork shoulder

1½ cups black pepper

2¼ cups brown sugar

2½ cups salt

12 oz. mustard seed

3 oz. paprika

3 oz. freezing pickle (also called pickle freeze)

4 oz. sodium nitrite

Cut the meat in chunks, mix together and sprinkle all the seasonings over meat. Mix thoroughly and run through the meat grinder on course grind, then repeat by grinding on fine grind. For best results, stuff in cleaned, natural hog casings, using string to tie off each end.

Use hardwood, preferably hickory or apple. Cool smoke (80–95°) will require a smoking process of 7–12 days. A hot smoke will vary by the smoking unit but an internal meat temperature of 165° is considered finished and a nice moist, lean product is the result.

Among hunters there probably isn't a more ego-involved topic than what constitutes a good sausage recipe. Naturally, I believe I have a real winner here and am happy to pass it along. This basic recipe was used by my grandfather and has been the basis of the family's sausage-making ritual for years. Given the quality of forage in the deer's diet and the extent of care taken in butchering and trimming, you may increase the percentage of venison in this recipe.

Venison Swiss Steak

2 lbs. venison loin or round steak
1 tablespoon dry mustard
¼ cup all-purpose flour
½ teaspoon salt
½ teaspoon freshly ground black pepper
2 tablespoons butter
2 cups baby carrots
1 medium onion, chopped
4 cups water
1 can diced tomatoes
2 tablespoons Worcestershire sauce

With a mallet or large knife pound meat to tenderize. Cut into serving-sized pieces. Combine mustard and flour and knead into the meat. Season with salt and pepper. Melt butter in a large frying pan. Add meat and brown on both sides. Add remaining ingredients, cook and simmer for 1½ hours.

Venison Swiss Steak is a mouth-watering treat that will tame that big mule deer or mountain elk.

Elk Chili

2 lbs. ground elk meat
4 tablespoons vegetable oil
1 large onion, chopped
1 green pepper, chopped
3 stalks celery, chopped
1 cup fresh mushrooms, sliced
6 medium ripe tomatoes, peeled and quartered
1 medium zucchini, cut into ½" cubes
1 32-oz. can V-8 juice
1 16-oz. can red kidney beans
1 16-oz. can chili beans
½ teaspoon chili powder
1 teaspoon ground cumin
1 6-oz. can tomato paste

Brown meat in vegetable oil in heavy frying pan over medium heat. Lightly sauté onion, green pepper, celery and mushrooms. Transfer to soup kettle, add remaining ingredients and simmer approximately 2 hours.

If mild chili is your choice, this recipe will satisfy.

Elk Curry

2 lbs. elk shoulder, bone, fat and sinew removed
4 tablespoons cooking oil
2 large onions, chopped
1 clove garlic, minced
2 stalks celery, chopped
1 teaspoon Worcestershire sauce
1 level tablespoon fresh curry
2 cups water
2 beef bouillon cubes

Cut meat into 1" cubes. Heat oil over medium heat in large frying pan. Add meat, onions, garlic and celery; stir and brown. Add Worcestershire sauce, curry, water and bouillon. Stir, cover and simmer for 30 minutes or until meat is tender. Serve over rice with hot fresh bread.

This stew variation will serve you well if you have a taste for curry.

Elk Fillets with Bleu Cheese Sauce

4 1"-thick fillets, cut from backstrap
2 cloves garlic, crushed
½ teaspoon freshly ground black pepper
4 tablespoons olive oil
1 oz. Jack Daniels bourbon

SAUCE
½ cup beef broth
¼ cup dry white wine
¼ cup bleu cheese

Mix crushed garlic with pepper and rub evenly into both sides of each steak. Pour olive oil and bourbon into a gallon-size sealable plastic bag, place steaks in the bag and turn to coat evenly. Let meat marinate for up to 3 hours.

Heat a large skillet (preferably cast iron) over medium-high heat. Add the steaks and cook 6–8 minutes on each side, turning only once. Remove meat from skillet and keep warm.

To make the sauce, blot out excess oil from pan with a paper towel. Over medium-high heat add broth and wine, stir and cook for approximately 2 minutes. Remove from heat and stir in bleu cheese, then spoon over steaks.

Serve with baked potato and steamed vegetables.

So many good recipes, so little time. This one could be a seasonal regular.

Elk Steak & Dumplings

2 lbs. loin steak, cut ¾" thick
1 cup flour
1 teaspoon black pepper
1 teaspoon salt
1 teaspoon seasoned salt
4 tablespoons vegetable oil
1 large onion, chopped
1 green pepper, chopped
1 cup fresh mushrooms, sliced
2 cups water
1 cup pea pods
2 beef bouillon cubes
2 tablespoons Worcestershire sauce
1 cup sour cream

Mix flour, pepper and salts; dredge meat and brown in oil in heavy frying pan. Add onion, green pepper and mushrooms when meat is turned. When meat is browned on both sides and onion is translucent add water, pea pods. bouillon and Worcestershire sauce; simmer for 30 minutes. Stir in sour cream. Serve over dumplings.

DUMPLINGS
8 slices wheat bread
2 tablespoons butter
1 tablespoon minced onion
1 teaspoon salt
2 eggs
½ cup cracker crumbs
1 teaspoon chopped parsley
dash of paprika, nutmeg, ginger

Soak bread in water; squeeze out water and pull apart in small chunks. Melt butter in large frying pan. Lightly sauté onion, add bread chunks and salt and brown lightly. Remove from heat, cool. Add remaining ingredients, mix well and form into balls about 1½" in diameter. Drop into boiling water, reduce heat and simmer for 10–12 minutes.

Elk Steak with Noodles

2 lbs. elk loin steak, cut ½" thick
½ cup flour
½ teaspoon salt
½ teaspoon black pepper
4 tablespoons vegetable oil
1 large onion, chopped
1 red pepper, chopped
6 tablespoons chili sauce
3 tablespoons Worcestershire sauce
1½ cups water
8 oz. noodles
¾ cup condensed cream of chicken soup
Parmesan cheese, grated

Cut steak into pieces that are approximately 2" x 2". Mix flour, salt and pepper. Dredge meat pieces and brown in oil in heavy frying pan over medium heat. Reduce heat, add onion, red pepper, chili sauce and Worcestershire sauce, cover and simmer for 30 minutes.

Meanwhile, cook and drain noodles. Heat condensed soup and toss with noodles.

Mound noodles, sprinkle with grated Parmesan cheese. Serve meat over noodles.

This is a family favorite. Although I don't always have elk meat on hand, I readily substitute white-tailed deer.

Elk Swiss Steak

2–3 lbs. elk round steak
⅓ cup flour
¼ teaspoon black pepper
¼ teaspoon seasoned salt
⅛ teaspoon garlic powder
4 tablespoons vegetable oil
1 large onion, chopped
1 green pepper, chopped
1 red pepper, chopped
6–8 fresh mushrooms, sliced
2 cups baby carrots
1 package Knorr vegetable soup mix
3 cups water
salt

Pound meat with a mallet or large knife. Mix flour, pepper, salt and garlic powder and dredge meat. Heat oil over medium-high heat in a large skillet and brown steaks. In a large cooking pot or Dutch oven layer meat with vegetables. Add soup mix and water and bring to a boil. Reduce heat and simmer for 1 hour, stirring occasionally. Thicken with remaining flour mixture and cook an additional 5 minutes. Salt to taste. Serve with mashed potatoes, baked squash and hot bread.

Whether you are walking back to camp or coming in from a long day outdoors, the wonderful aroma of Swiss Steak slowly cooking will quicken your pace and stir your appetite.

Buffalo Meatballs

2 lbs. ground buffalo
½ teaspoon salt
¼ teaspoon black pepper
¼ teaspoon seasoned salt
2 cups bread crumbs
¼ cup milk
2 eggs, beaten
1 medium onion, minced
1 package Lipton onion and mushroom soup mix

In large bowl combine all ingredients except soup mix and roll into 1" balls. Bake in oven on greased pan at 325° for approximately 25 minutes.

Make gravy from soup mix following directions on package for the gravy recipe.

Lean, wholesome and tasty, these meatballs can be served with mashed potatoes, rice or pasta and will surely satisfy.

Wyoming Pronghorn Chili

2 lbs. ground antelope or venison
2 tablespoons vegetable oil
1 large onion, chopped
1 green pepper, chopped
1 32-oz. can stewed tomatoes
1 46-oz. can tomato juice
1 12-oz. can tomato paste
1 32-oz. can chili beans
1 16-oz. can kidney beans
1 12-oz. can beer
1 cup black olives, sliced
¼ cup brown sugar
2 tablespoons Worcestershire sauce
1 teaspoon salt
½ teaspoon black pepper
1 tablespoon chili powder

Brown meat in vegetable oil in a heavy frying pan over medium-high heat. Lightly sauté onion and green pepper. Transfer meat, onion and pepper to soup kettle, add remaining ingredients to kettle and simmer, covered, for 1–2 hours.

Serve with thick slices of sourdough or beer bread.

I had a buddy who lived with fear and danger. Occasionally she let him go hunting.

Wild Sides

A Few Helpful Hints about Wild Rice

Wild rice will grace "something wild" like ice cream will complement apple pie. Wild rice is a versatile grain with uses limited only by one's imagination. I use it freely with many recipes and have even experimented with wild rice in pancakes, muffins and biscuits. Cooked or steamed it is high in carbohydrates, low in fat and contains essential protein.

About Wild Rice

Wild rice is a self-perpetuating wild plant that has grown naturally in lakes, rivers and the marsh areas of our beautiful North Country for centuries. Native Americans harvested the smoky reed during autumn rituals and used it as a staple in much of their cooking. As wild rice grew in popularity in North American cooking, the demand has been met with commercial growing and harvesting. Paddy grown (non-native) rice is generally labeled as such, is darker in color and tends to be less expensive. Wild rice is versatile, easy to prepare and the smoky richness of its natural flavor will enhance the presentation of meats and fish for a nutritious dining delight.

To Prepare Wild Rice

For 4 cups of cooked rice, rinse 1 cup of wild rice and drain. In a kettle or large saucepan, bring 4 cups of water and 1 teaspoon of salt to a rolling boil. Slowly add the rice, reduce heat to low, cover and cook for 50 minutes to 1 hour or until kernels are popped, fluffy and tender. Drain excess water. Wild rice will take an hour to prepare so I generally double the amount I need and freeze the extra for use with future meals. To enhance flavor, add chicken or beef bouillon to the water during cooking. Minced or chopped onions, peppers, carrots, celery, mushrooms and garlic, sautéed in butter and added to the rice at the end of the cooking process, will enrich the flavor and appearance of your dish. You can add wild rice to just about any slow cooker, crock pot or Dutch oven recipe with unique results.

Baking Powder Biscuits

2 cups unbleached flour
1 tablespoon baking powder
2 teaspoons sugar
1 teaspoon salt
⅓ cup vegetable shortening
⅔ cup milk
1 tablespoon melted butter

Preheat oven to 450°. In a medium bowl sift together the flour, baking powder, sugar and salt. Cut in shortening until the mixture resembles coarse meal. Gradually stir in enough milk to make a soft, puffy, pliable dough. Too much milk will make dough sticky.

Turn the dough out onto a lightly floured surface. Knead lightly, about 6 times. Roll out into a circle ½" thick. Brush surface with the melted butter. Fold the dough and again roll out into a circle ½" thick. Cut out biscuits using 2" cutter. Place in the middle of the oven on an ungreased baking sheet. Bake for 10–12 minutes or until golden.

I grew up eating these biscuits, usually topped with homemade jelly or honey. A wonderful childhood memory.

Buttermilk Biscuits

2 cups flour, divided
1 tablespoon baking powder
1 teaspoon salt
⅓ cup shortening
⅔ cup buttermilk

Preheat oven to 400°. In a medium bowl combine 1½ cups flour, baking powder and salt. Cut in the shortening until the mixture resembles coarse meal. Stir in the buttermilk until blended. Turn dough out on a floured surface and knead in the remaining flour. Roll out the dough ½" thick. Cut into 2" circles with cutter. Place on a greased baking sheet and bake 10–12 minutes or until golden.

Light and fluffy, these biscuits go well with stew or any dish served with a rich gravy.

Cheese Biscuits

2 cups flour
1 tablespoon baking powder
½ teaspoon salt
¼ teaspoon garlic powder
2 cups cream
½ cup grated cheddar cheese

Preheat oven to 375°. In a medium bowl combine flour, baking powder, salt and garlic powder. Slowly add cream, stir until moistened. Blend in grated cheddar cheese. Drop by tablespoonfuls on a greased baking sheet. Bake for 12–15 minutes or until golden.

Try these biscuits with fish or fowl and revel in the compliments.

Herb Biscuits

2 cups flour
1 tablespoon baking powder
¼ cup sugar
½ teaspoon salt
1 tablespoon chopped parsley
1 teaspoon chopped chives
½ teaspoon chopped thyme
2 cups cream

Preheat the oven to 375°. In a medium bowl, combine flour, baking powder, sugar, salt, parsley, chives and thyme. Slowly stir in the cream until moistened. Drop by tablespoonfuls on a greased baking sheet. Bake for 12–15 minutes or until golden.

When you bake these biscuits, make a double batch and put some in an airtight bag for lunch on a future hunting or fishing trip.

Wheat Bran Biscuits

1½ cups all-purpose flour
½ cup wheat bran
2 tablespoons sugar
1 tablespoon baking powder
¼ teaspoon salt
½ cup shortening
1 egg
½ cup milk
1 tablespoon butter, melted

Preheat the oven to 425°. In a large bowl, combine flour, bran, sugar, baking powder and salt. Cut in shortening until crumbly. Beat egg and milk, stir into flour mixture, forming a ball. Turn onto a floured surface and knead several times. Roll to a thickness of ½" and brush with melted butter. Cut with biscuit cutter or a glass. Bake on an ungreased baking sheet for 10–12 minutes or until golden.

Wholesome and hearty, loaded with fiber (and that's a good thing).

Cranberry Muffins

½ stick butter
½ cup sugar
2 eggs
2¼ cups all-purpose flour
2 teaspoons baking powder
½ teaspoon salt
1 cup eggnog
1 cup cranberries, chopped
⅓ cup chopped pecans

Preheat oven to 350°. Cream butter and sugar, beat in eggs. Combine flour, baking powder and salt. Add flour mixture and eggnog to butter and sugar mixture, mix well. Add cranberries and pecans. Fill paper-lined muffin cups ¾ full. Bake 18–20 minutes or until golden.

Chock-full of nuts and berries, these muffins served warm at breakfast will sustain any hunter between meals.

Huckleberry Muffins

2½ cups flour
2 teaspoons baking powder
2 teaspoons baking soda
1 teaspoon salt
1 cup raw wheat bran
1 cup boiling water
2 eggs
1¼ cup sugar
¾ cup vegetable oil
2 cups buttermilk
1 cup fresh huckleberries

In small bowl combine flour, baking powder, baking soda and salt.

In a separate small bowl combine the wheat bran and water, mixing to ensure that water is absorbed.

In large bowl, lightly beat eggs, sugar, oil and buttermilk, stir in bran. Add the flour mixture and stir only until moistened. Lightly fold in the huckleberries. Chill the batter for several hours.

Preheat oven to 350°. Spoon chilled batter into greased muffin pans. Bake for 25–30 minutes or until golden.

Makes 12 muffins.

These muffins can be baked at home and taken along on any trip. Eaten with coffee on a long drive, in the boat or duck blind, they augment the day and keep hunger pangs at bay.

Banana Oat Bran Muffins

3 medium bananas, mashed
2 egg whites
⅓ cup vegetable oil
¾ teaspoon salt
½ cup sugar
1 cup flour
2 teaspoons baking powder
¼ teaspoon baking soda
½ cup oat bran
¼ cup toasted wheat germ
½ cup walnuts, chopped
½ cup dates, chopped

Heat oven to 350°. In medium bowl combine banana, egg whites and oil. Sift together salt, sugar, flour, baking powder and baking soda. Mix in all ingredients all at once and stir only until flour is moistened. The batter will be lumpy. Fill muffin cups or greased muffin tins ¾ full and bake 20–25 minutes or until golden.

Sealed in an airtight container, these muffins will stay fresh, moist and delicious until the last one is eaten.

Buckwheat Pancakes

½ cup buckwheat flour
½ cup unbleached all-purpose flour
¼ cup whole wheat flour
¼ cup ground almonds
2 tablespoons baking powder
½ teaspoon salt
2 eggs, separated
1 cup milk
2 tablespoons cooking oil

Mix together dry ingredients in medium bowl. In small bowl beat egg yolks, milk and cooking oil until well blended. Pour into the dry ingredients and stir until blended. Beat egg whites until stiff, fold into batter.

Lightly oil the griddle and heat over low or medium heat. Use about 3 tablespoons of batter per cake. Cook until several bubbles break the top, then turn and cook about a minute on the second side.

For those who enjoy the unique taste of buckwheat, these pancakes are made to order.

Potato Pancakes

½ cup milk
3 eggs
4½ cups grated potatoes
1 small onion, grated
4½ tablespoons flour
1½ teaspoons salt
½ teaspoon baking powder

Mix all ingredients. Lightly oil griddle over medium heat. Pour on 2–3 tablespoons batter per cake. Cook until golden, turning once.

Memories of my father quickly surface when these golden cakes are served. In the days before blenders I remember him grating the potatoes by hand, adding to the procedure and drawing out the anticipation.

Sour Cream Pancakes

½ cup sour cream
½ cup skim milk
2 eggs, separated
1 cup flour
1 teaspoon baking powder
1 tablespoon sugar
½ teaspoon salt
½ cup cooking oil

Mix sour cream, milk and egg yolks in a medium bowl. Add flour, baking powder, sugar and salt and mix. Add cooking oil and stir until smooth. Beat egg whites until stiff and fold into batter. Heat a lightly greased griddle over low or medium heat. Use 3 tablespoons batter per cake.

Cook until several bubbles break the surface of the cake, then flip and cook about a minute on the second side.

No breakfast is complete without cakes. These light, fluffy pancakes will help stoke the day ahead.

Buttered Crumb Noodles

6 cups water
3 chicken bouillon cubes
8 oz. wide noodles
1 slice whole wheat bread, toasted, crumbed
4 tablespoons butter, divided
salt and pepper

Bring water with bouillon to a boil. Add noodles, cook 8–10 minutes or until tender. Sauté bread crumbs in 1 tablespoon butter until lightly browned.

Drain noodles, but do not rinse. Return noodles to original kettle, add remaining butter, salt and pepper to taste. Add bread crumbs.

A simple, tasty addition to any game meal.

Potato Dumplings

2 eggs
1 cup flour, divided
½ cup dried bread crumbs
½ teaspoon salt
½ teaspoon seasoned salt
1 teaspoon ground nutmeg
1 teaspoon fresh minced parsley
4 cups mashed potatoes

In a large bowl, combine eggs, ¾ cup flour, bread crumbs and seasonings. Add potatoes and blend thoroughly. Shape into golf ball-sized dumplings and roll in remaining flour. In a large kettle or soup pot bring salted water to a boil. Add several dumplings at a time. Simmer, uncovered, until dumplings rise to the top. Cook 3 minutes longer. Remove to bowl and serve with sauerbraten and gravy or goulash.

Another simple, tasty recipe from my childhood worth repeating. It's a time-consuming process but oh, so, good and well worth the effort.

Baked Corn

1 can whole-kernel corn, drained
1 can cream-style corn
½ cup cornmeal
1 small onion, chopped
2 cloves garlic, crushed
1 4-oz. can green chilies
1 sweet red pepper, chopped
2 cups grated cheddar cheese
1 teaspoon baking powder
¼ cup corn oil
2 eggs, beaten

In a Dutch oven or cast iron bean pot, blend all ingredients. Cover and bake at 350° for 45–50 minutes.

Quick and easy to prepare ahead of time. This simple meal lets the oven or fire do the work before it's served.

Camp Cook's Onion Soup

6 large onions, chopped
½ cup butter
6 10.5-oz. cans condensed beef broth
1½ teaspoons Worcestershire sauce
3 bay leaves
8 1"-thick slices French bread, toasted
1 cup shredded Parmesan cheese
1 cup shredded mozzarella cheese

In a large skillet over medium heat sauté onions in butter until tender. Transfer to a 5-qt. crock pot. Add broth, Worcestershire sauce and bay leaves. Cover and cook on low for 5–7 hours. Discard bay leaves. Ladle soup into individual bowls and top each with a piece of toasted French bread sprinkled with cheese.

Hot, savory, delicious. This popular soup can be served with an accompanying meal or stand alone for a light lunch.

Camp Kitchen Eggs

1 loaf French or Italian bread
1 lb. smoked venison country-style sausage
1 small onion, diced
2 tablespoons diced red pepper
1 cup cream
8 oz. grated sharp cheddar cheese
8–10 large eggs

Preheat oven to 350°. Lightly grease or use cooking spray to coat a 9x13 baking pan. Slice the bread 1" thick and place in the bottom of the pan. Slice the sausage ⅛" thick and layer evenly on bread. Sprinkle with onion and red pepper. In a medium bowl, add cream and cheese to eggs and beat thoroughly. Pour mixture over the layers in baking pan and bake for 35 minutes.

In my deer camp we have two meals. Brunch at 10:30 and supper after sundown. These camp eggs are served with pancakes and sausage at least once each season.

Campfire Veggies

6 medium potatoes, sliced
2 large onions, sliced
1 bag baby carrots
1 sweet red pepper, chopped
1 medium zucchini, sliced
1 can sliced mushrooms
1 can whole-kernel corn
1 can whole tomatoes
1 teaspoon salt
½ teaspoon black pepper

Place all of the fresh vegetables in a large Dutch oven or roaster. Add canned vegetables with juice, salt and pepper. Cook over hot coals 2–4 hours or in an oven at 350° for 1½ hours.

Put it all together and set it on the fire. This allows you to tend to the steaks or whatever else may be on the menu.

Campsite Beans

1 lb. ground venison
½ lb. bacon, sliced
1 large onion, chopped
1 16-oz. can pork & beans
1 16-oz. can kidney beans
1 16-oz. can Bush's baked beans
¾ cup brown sugar
½ cup ketchup
2 teaspoons vinegar
1 teaspoon hot & spicy mustard

In a large Dutch oven or cast iron bean pot, brown the venison and bacon over medium-high heat. Add remaining ingredients and slow cook over the campfire, stirring occasionally, for 2 hours. When baking in the oven, bake at 325° for 1½ hours.

Another side dish you can put together, then let the fire do the work while you tend to your main course.

Grilled Mushrooms

1 lb. large fresh mushrooms
¼ cup lemon juice
3 tablespoons fresh parsley, minced
2 tablespoons olive oil
3 large cloves garlic, crushed
¼ teaspoons black pepper

Skewer mushrooms or use a grilling basket. In a small bowl combine all remaining ingredients and set side. Grill the mushrooms approximately 4 minutes 4–5" above heat source, basting generously with the lemon garlic blend. Turn and continue grilling 4–6 minutes or until tender. Use remaining blend to baste before serving.

A nice, tasty addition to any camp meal.

Roasted Veggies

8–10 small red potatoes, quartered
4 medium carrots, sliced
2 turnips, peeled and cubed
2 cloves garlic, minced
4 tablespoons olive oil
1 tablespoon dry onion soup mix
½ teaspoon salt
¼ teaspoon black pepper

Place the potatoes, carrots, turnips and garlic in a large bowl. Add olive oil, soup mix, salt and pepper and toss to coat. Transfer veggies to a 9x13 baking dish. Bake uncovered at 350° for 40 minutes. Increase heat to 450° and bake an additional 10 minutes or until veggies are tender.

Served with country-style ribs or grilled halibut steaks, these grilled veggies will add another dimension to your meal.

Skillet Rice

1 lb. ground pork sausage
1 medium onion, chopped
½ cup chopped red pepper
1 cup sliced fresh mushrooms
¾ cup water
1 chicken bouillon cube
⅛ teaspoon black pepper
¾ cup instant rice
¼ cup shredded Parmesan cheese

In a large skillet, fry sausage over medium-high heat. Add onion and red pepper when meat is turned. Add mushrooms, water, bouillon and pepper, bring to a boil. Add rice and reduce heat. Cover and simmer for 5 minutes or until rice is tender. Sprinkle with Parmesan cheese and serve.

A complete meal or as a side with grilled venison steaks, this creation will add flavor and color to your dinner.

Squash Casserole

4 cups squash, baked and cooled
¾ cup sugar
3 eggs
½ cup cream
2 teaspoons vanilla
4 tablespoons margarine, melted

In large bowl beat all ingredients until smooth. Put in 9x13 baking dish.

TOPPING
½ cup brown sugar
½ cup flour
½ stick margarine

Mix brown sugar with flour and sprinkle over top of squash mixture. Melt margarine and drizzle over the top.

Bake at 325° for 1 hour.

For several years I hunted on a ranch where I was welcome to spend the night. The ranch wife cooked some fabulous meals. This was one of my favorites.

Stuffed Acorn Squash

1 acorn squash, halved lengthwise, seeds removed
4 tablespoons butter
1 cup diced celery
1 cup chopped onion
1 cup fresh mushrooms
2 cups seasoned croutons
1 teaspoon chopped parsley
salt and pepper to taste
½ cup shredded cheddar cheese

Preheat oven to 350°. Place squash cut side down in a glass baking dish. Microwave on high for 10–12 minutes or until almost tender. While squash is in the microwave, melt the butter over medium-high heat in a frying pan. Add celery, onions and mushrooms and sauté gently. Add croutons, parsley, salt and pepper and blend. Place half the mixture into each squash cavity, cover with foil and bake in oven for 20 minutes. Remove foil, sprinkle with cheese and return to the oven for several minutes or until cheese bubbles.

Of all the veggies available, I like squash the best and it seems to compliment wild game like no other. I serve this stuffed squash several times each year and always get positive reviews.

Sweet & Sour Beans

6 slices bacon, diced
2 onions, chopped
1 stalk celery, chopped
2 cloves garlic, crushed
1 cup brown sugar
½ cup cider vinegar
1 tablespoon hot & spicy mustard
1 teaspoon salt
1 28-oz. can Bush's baked beans
1 16-oz. can red kidney beans
1 16-oz. can pinto beans
1 16-oz. can black-eyed peas

In a large skillet over medium-high heat, fry bacon until crisp. Remove bacon from the pan and sauté onions, celery and garlic until tender. Add brown sugar, vinegar, mustard and salt. Stir and cook until mixture starts to bubble. Transfer mixture to a slow cooker or crock pot, add the bacon, all of the beans and black-eyed peas and stir to blend. Cover and cook on high heat for 3–4 hours.

Simple to make, rich in flavor and substance. Serve this dish with any fish or game.

Sweet Onion Casserole

4 tablespoons butter
5–6 large sweet (Vidalia) onions, sliced ¼" thick
1 sweet red pepper, chopped
⅓ cup sour cream
½ teaspoon seasoned salt
¾ cup grated Parmesan cheese
12 Keebler butter crackers, crushed

In a large skillet over medium-high heat melt butter and gently sauté the sliced onions and red pepper until tender. Remove from heat, stir in the sour cream, seasoned salt and Parmesan cheese. Transfer to a 1-qt. baking dish, sprinkle with crushed crackers and bake at 350° for 20 minutes.

Sweet onions make the best casserole, and Vidalias are the best of the best. This side will be a welcome addition to any meal.

Twice-Baked Campfire Potatoes

4 large baking potatoes
3 tablespoons butter, divided
1 small onion, minced
¾ cup evaporated milk
½ teaspoon seasoned salt
1 tablespoon parsley flakes
1 cup grated cheddar cheese

Wash potatoes, pierce each with a knife and rub with about a tablespoon of butter. Wrap individually in foil and bake in the coals for 1 hour, turning occasionally. Remove potatoes from foil, cut in half lengthwise and scoop out the insides, leaving some meat on the skin to form a nice shell. Set the shells aside. In a bowl, mash the potatoes, add remaining butter, onion, milk, salt, parsley flakes and cheese and blend thoroughly. Spoon the mixture back into the shells and place in a hot Dutch oven for an additional 15 minutes to finish baking. Makes a nice addition to any camp meal.

Camp cooking never tasted so good. Serve it up with grilled fish, fowl or venison and your guests will stuff themselves beyond comfort.

Unlucky Hunter Hotdish

3 lbs. potatoes, peeled, cooked and mashed
1 head cabbage, chopped and cooked
½ teaspoon seasoned salt
¼ teaspoon pepper
1 stick butter
3 lbs. ground pork sausage
2 large onions, chopped
2 cups Italian seasoned croutons

Blend the cooked mashed potatoes with the cooked cabbage, season with salt and pepper. Melt the butter in a large skillet and brown the meat. Add the onion and cook an additional 3–5 minutes, then add the croutons. Combine the meat mixture with the potato and cabbage mixture, turn into a large greased baking pan and press firmly. Cover with foil and bake at 375° for 1 hour.

This will feed about six hungry hunters who were dreaming of fresh venison steaks. Although some days are better than others, my camp has never had to resort to roughing it like this, but I suppose one day it may be possible.

Wild Rice & Corn Chowder

¼ **cup butter**
⅓ **cup wild rice, uncooked**
½ **cup diced carrots**
½ **cup diced celery**
1 **cup corn**
1 **medium onion, diced**
½ **cup flour**
5 **cups chicken stock**
1 **cup cream**
½ **teaspoon salt**
¼ **teaspoon white pepper**

In a 3-qt. saucepan, melt butter over medium heat and add rice, carrots, celery, corn and onion. Sauté lightly for 3–4 minutes, then add flour and stir well. Add chicken stock and simmer for 40 minutes. Add cream, salt and pepper and continue to simmer an additional 15 minutes or until rice is done.

Liven up your camp cooking with this simple chowder. Served as a side to any game or fish, it is sure to create an aura of satisfaction and contentment.

Wild Rice Soup

8 cups water, divided
1 teaspoon basil
1 cup wild rice, uncooked
3 tablespoons butter
1 carrot, chopped
1 onion, minced
1 stalk celery, chopped
1 small sweet red pepper, chopped
5–6 chicken bouillon cubes
1 pint cream
dash each of sage and thyme
salt and pepper to taste

Combine 4 cups water and basil in a large soup kettle, bring to a boil and add rice. Reduce heat, cover and simmer for 45 minutes.

While rice is cooking, melt butter in a large frying pan over medium heat. Add carrot, onion, celery and red pepper and sauté until lightly browned. Add the veggies to the rice in the soup kettle and add the additional water, bouillon, cream, sage, thyme, salt and pepper. Simmer for an additional 20 minutes.

Long on tradition and flavor, a pot of wild rice soup on the stove or in the crock pot will greet any hunter who heads back to the cabin.

Wild Rice Stuffing

4 cups water
4 chicken bouillon cubes
1 cup wild rice, uncooked
4 slices bacon, diced
4 tablespoons butter
1 onion, chopped
2 stalks celery, chopped
1 cup sliced mushrooms
3 cups seasoned croutons
¼ teaspoon sage
salt and pepper to taste

Bring water and bouillon to a boil in large saucepan. Add rice, reduce heat and cover. Cook for approximately 50 minutes or until rice kernels have popped and are tender.

Fry bacon slices with butter, onion, celery and mushrooms in a large frying pan until lightly browned. Remove from heat, add croutons and seasonings. Mix with the cooked wild rice. Allow to cool before stuffing a bird.

Used to stuff a bird cavity or spread in a baking dish, this stuffing will be a hit in any kitchen for any occasion.

INDEX

About the Author

Richard Gauerke will rarely pass on an opportunity to hunt, fish or cook. Bonding with nature at an early age, he has developed a strong respect for all God's creatures and is passionate about the outdoors and the world around him. A glimpse at his back trail reveals over five decades of beautiful sunrises, bone-chilling mornings, hot coffee on the camp stove, stew in the pot and lots of friends—friends with hearty appetites and adventure in their souls.

Those many friends will attest that a venture into the wilds with Richard is an experience due to his creative and delicious comfort food. Richard believes an integral part of each adventure is the food. Therefore, each meal or snack is anticipated with delight. Whether it's the crew at the gun club or the fellas in fish camp, Richard and his buddies love good food and they eat well.

As a popular camp cook, Richard's cooking and recipes were much sought after; it was this interest that led to the creation of his first book, *The Best of the Prairie*, which was soon followed by two more. Richard enjoys demonstrating his cooking skills whether in his kitchen or at a campsite, and he is on a continuous quest for new and tasty recipes.